WHISPERS FROM THE MURDER FARM: THE CASE OF BELLE GUNNESS

Inside the Mind of America's Darkest Femme Fatale

SHADOWS OF THE PAST
BOOK III

ELIZA HAWTHORNE

Copyright © 2024 by Cordova Consulting

All rights reserved. This publication, including its content, design, and structure, is protected by copyright law, a crucial aspect that should not be overlooked. It is of utmost importance to respect this law. No part of this publication may be reproduced, stored, or transmitted in any form or by any means, electronic, mechanical, photocopying, recording, scanning, or otherwise, without written permission from the publisher. To obtain such permission, please contact the publisher directly. It is illegal to copy this book, post it to a website, or distribute it by any other means without permission. We urge you to be aware of and responsible for your actions in relation to this law.

The author of this work asserts their moral right to be identified as such, a testament to their unwavering dedication and boundless creativity. This includes the right to prevent any distortion, mutilation, or other modification of their work that would be prejudicial to their honor or reputation. We ask for your respect and appreciation for the author's rights in this matter.

While the author strives to ensure the accuracy and relevance of the content, they cannot guarantee the persistence or accuracy of URLs for external or third-party Internet websites referred to in this publication. It is important to note that they do not guarantee that any content on such Websites is, or will remain, accurate or appropriate, and users should exercise caution when accessing such content. We want to ensure that you are well-informed and exercise caution when using external links.

Designations used by companies to distinguish their products are often claimed as trademarks. All brand names and product names used in this book and on its cover are trade names, service marks, trademarks, and registered trademarks of their respective owners. A trade name is a name a company uses to identify itself, while a service mark is a type of trademark that identifies a service rather than a product. A trademark is a symbol, word, or word legally registered or established by use as representing a company or product. A registered trademark is a trademark that has been officially registered with a government agency. The publishers and the book are not associated with any product or vendor mentioned in this book.

None of the companies referenced within the book have endorsed the book.

TABLE OF CONTENTS

Introduction — vii

1. THE EARLY YEARS — 1
   Childhood in Norway — 2
   Family Dynamics and Early Influences — 5
   The Immigrant Dream — 7
   Settling in America — 9

2. THE MAKING OF A MURDERER — 13
   Life in Chicago — 13
   The First Marriage: Mads Sorenson — 16
   The Insurance Payout — 18
   The Move to La Porte, Indiana — 20

3. THE MURDER FARM — 23
   Acquiring the Farm — 23
   The First Victims — 26
   The Role of Personal Ads — 29
   The Disappearance of Suitors — 31

4. METHODS OF MURDER — 35
   Poisoning Techniques — 35
   The Use of Blunt Force — 38
   Disposal Methods — 41
   The Role of Accomplices — 44

5. GENDER DYNAMICS AND SOCIETAL NORMS — 47
   Women's Roles in Early 1900s America — 47
   Belle as a Femme Fatale — 50
   Media Portrayal of Female Criminals — 52
   Public Reaction and Scandal — 54

6. FORENSIC CHALLENGES — 57
   Early 20th Century Forensics — 57
   The Role of Autopsies — 62
   Identifying the Victims — 64
   Modern Forensic Comparisons — 66

7. THE INVESTIGATION 69
   The Initial Discovery 69
   The Role of Ray Lamphere 72
   The House Fire 74
   Digging up the Farm 77

8. TRIALS AND LEGAL PROCEEDINGS 81
   Ray Lamphere's Trial 81
   Testimonies and Evidence 84
   The Verdict 86
   Public and Media Reaction 88

9. THE MYSTERY OF BELLE'S DEATH 91
   The Burned Body 91
   Escape Theories 94
   Sightings and Rumors 96
   Modern Investigations 98

10. PSYCHOLOGICAL PROFILE 101
    Early Psychological Signs 101
    Narcissism and Psychopathy 103
    Financial Motivations 106
    Expert Analysis and Diagnoses 108

11. COMPARATIVE ANALYSIS 111
    H. H. Holmes 112
    Jane Toppan 114
    The Axeman of New Orleans 117
    Gender Comparisons in Serial Killing . . 119

12. LEGACY AND IMPACT 123
    Media Legacy 123
    Influence on True Crime Literature 126
    Belle Gunness in Popular Culture 128
    Lessons Learned and Modern Reflections . . 130

    Conclusion 133
    Book Club Discussion Questions: Shadows of the Past - Belle Gunness 137
    References 141
    About the Author 145
    Also by Eliza Hawthorne 147
    Also by Publisher Cordova Consulting . . 149

INTRODUCTION

The sun had barely risen on April 28, 1908, when the smoldering ruins of Belle Gunness's farmhouse greeted the eyes of her neighbors and the local authorities in La Porte, Indiana. Smoke curled into the sky, carrying with it the acrid scent of charred wood and the unmistakable stench of burnt flesh. The first responders, eyes wide with horror, stumbled upon a scene that would haunt them for years. The farmhouse, once a symbol of rural tranquility, had transformed into a grotesque monument to death.

As they sifted through the ashes, the full extent of the horror began to reveal itself. Bodies—some intact, some mere fragments—were unearthed from the blackened debris. The smell of decay mingled with the scent of smoke, creating an almost unbearable miasma. It was a scene of utter chaos and disbelief, where every shovelful of dirt revealed yet another gruesome secret.

At the center of this macabre tableau stood Belle Gunness, the seemingly respectable widow whose farm concealed unimaginable horrors. Belle was an immigrant from Norway who had come to America seeking a better life. She settled in La Porte, Indiana, and transformed her farm into a lucrative enterprise. But beneath her facade of respectability lay a calculated and ruthless killer.

Belle's background was as complex as it was tragic. Born in Norway, she immigrated to the United States in the late 19th century. She married twice, both husbands meeting untimely and suspicious ends. After their deaths, Belle used her farm to lure wealthy men, promising them love and prosperity. Instead, they met brutal deaths, their bodies buried in shallow graves on her property.

Belle Gunness was a psychological enigma. Her actions defied the gender norms of her time, challenging the societal expectations placed upon women. The pressures of immigrant life, coupled with her own ambitions and desires, may have driven her to commit such heinous acts. She was a master manipulator, able to hide her true nature while presenting herself as a grieving widow and loving mother.

The sheer number of victims is staggering. Estimates suggest that Belle may have killed as many as 40 people, including her own children. Her methods were cold and calculated. She used poison, blunt force, and fire to dispatch her victims, ensuring their wealth became hers. Belle's ability to manipulate public perception allowed her to evade suspicion for years. She hid in plain sight, her crimes undetected by a society ill-equipped to recognize a female serial killer.

The early 20th century presented significant forensic and societal limitations. The science of criminal investigation was still in its infancy. Forensic techniques we take for granted today were nonexistent or rudimentary at best. These limitations allowed Belle to continue her murderous activities with little fear of capture.

The forensic limitations were further compounded by the societal attitudes of the time. The idea that a woman, especially a widow and mother, could be capable of such heinous acts was inconceivable to many. This gender bias in criminal investigations played directly into Belle's hands, allowing her to slip under the radar. Early law enforcement, with its patriarchal assumptions, often failed to consider women as serious criminal threats, especially in cases involving violent murders. In this environment, Belle thrived, her crimes met with disbelief rather than scrutiny. It was not just her manipulation of individuals, but her manipulation of societal norms that kept her hidden in plain sight.

Exploring Belle Gunness's case through a historical and psychological lens provides valuable insights. It allows us to understand the societal and forensic challenges of early 20th-century America. It also offers a window into the mind of a woman who defied all expectations, committing crimes that shocked the world.

From a psychological standpoint, Belle Gunness exhibited traits that modern experts might associate with psychopathy and narcissism. Her ability to maintain an outwardly normal life while committing such atrocities speaks to her skill in manipulating those around her. She operated without empathy, viewing her victims as mere pawns in her pursuit of wealth. The sheer coldness of her actions—luring men to their deaths, even killing her own children—suggests a mind capable of compartmentalizing guilt, driven by personal ambition and survival at any cost. This psychological complexity invites us to question the origins of such behavior: was it her upbringing, the pressures of immigration, or an inherent darkness that pushed her to these acts?

This book aims to provide an in-depth understanding of Belle Gunness's life, crimes, and the societal challenges of her time. We will delve into her psychological profile using modern forensic and psychological analysis. Through Belle's story, we will explore early forensic science, gender roles, and criminal psychology. Readers will feel shock, empathy, and reflection as they journey through the twisted tale of the Murder Farm.

In addition to unraveling the mystery of Belle's crimes, this book also examines the broader societal implications of her actions. At a time when women were expected to be nurturing and passive, Belle's life was a stark contrast to the gender norms of her era. Her ability to subvert these expectations speaks to the power dynamics at play, both in her personal life and in the criminal activities she masterminded. How did a woman from a small Norwegian town rise to infamy as one of America's most prolific killers? And how did the male-dominated society she lived in, one that underestimated women, allow her to operate for so long? These are questions that resonate even today, as we continue to explore the intersections of gender, power, and criminality.

Each chapter of this book offers a piece of the puzzle:

1. **Belle's Background**: Her early life in Norway and immigration to the U.S.
2. **The Murder Farm**: How she used the farm to lure and kill wealthy men.
3. **Victims and Methods**: Belle's manipulative tactics and calculated killings.
4. **Gender Dynamics**: How her actions defied societal norms of the time.
5. **Forensic Challenges**: The limitations in investigative techniques and comparisons to modern methods.
6. **Mystery of Her Death**: Theories surrounding her escape and possible death.
7. **Psychological Profile**: An analysis of her mental state using modern psychology.

The logical flow of this narrative takes you from Belle's early life to the grim discoveries on her farm, the ensuing investigation, and her lasting legacy. As you read, I encourage you to question how societal pressures and personal ambitions can shape a criminal mind. Speculate on Belle's guilt or innocence in specific incidents, fostering a deeper engagement with the narrative.

This is more than a historical account. It is an invitation to ponder the complexities of human nature. It is a call to understand how a seemingly respectable widow could hide such darkness. As you turn the pages, you will find yourself drawn into a world where the lines between good and evil blur, and the true nature of Belle Gunness remains an enigma.

Whispers from the Murder Farm is the third installment in the *Shadows of the Past* series, a collection dedicated to unraveling history's most chilling and unresolved cases. Each book in this series invites readers to step into the shoes of a different notorious figure, peeling back the layers of mystery surrounding their lives and crimes. As part of this ongoing journey through forgotten shadows, this book builds on the previous investigations and delves deeper into the psychological and societal frameworks that shaped these figures. So, as you begin this chapter of the series, keep in mind that this story is just one piece of a larger exploration of history's most perplexing cold cases.

So, dear reader, prepare yourself for a journey into the mind of America's darkest femme fatale. The story of Belle Gunness is one of horror, mystery, and profound psychological complexity. It is a tale that will captivate your imagination and challenge your understanding of human nature. The adventure begins now.

CHAPTER 1
THE EARLY YEARS

In the quiet, rugged landscape of Selbu, Norway, on a cold November day in 1859, Brynhild Paulsdatter Storset was born into a world of stark contrast and harsh realities. Life in Selbu was a daily struggle against the elements and economic hardship. The Storset family, like many others in the region, grappled with poverty. They worked tirelessly just to keep food on the table and a roof over their heads. Brynhild, who would later become known to the world as Belle Gunness, grew up in this challenging environment, shaping the complex and dark persona she would later become.

The harsh Norwegian winters only compounded these difficulties. Blizzards and biting winds would sweep down from the mountains, isolating families like the Storsets for weeks at a time. Crops were often meager, leaving the family to rely on what little they could store from the short growing season. The cold seeped into every part of their lives, a constant reminder of nature's indifference to human struggle. In this environment, survival meant resilience, and it was here that Brynhild learned to endure both the harshness of the land and the unyielding expectations of her family.

CHILDHOOD IN NORWAY

Selbu, nestled in the heart of Norway, was a place where the rugged mountains met the fertile valleys. It was a land of stark beauty but also of unrelenting hardship. Born as Brynhild Paulsdatter Storset, Belle's early years were marked by the relentless grind of poverty. Her family, like many others in the area, relied on subsistence farming. They toiled from dawn to dusk, eking out a meager existence from the unforgiving soil. Brynhild, the young girl who would grow into a notorious serial killer, spent her childhood amidst this struggle, a struggle that would shape her in ways unimaginable.

The soil itself seemed resistant to the idea of prosperity. Rocky, thin, and hard to cultivate, it yielded little, despite the long hours of backbreaking work. Belle's father, Paul, was unrelenting in his insistence that his children contribute fully to the labor, often pushing them past their limits. In these conditions, the children were expected to grow up quickly, leaving little room for a carefree childhood. This environment not only shaped Belle's work ethic but also instilled in her the cold pragmatism that would later characterize her actions.

From an early age, Brynhild worked on the family farm. The labor was grueling, and the rewards were scant. She learned to milk cows, tend to crops, and perform the myriad tasks required to keep the farm running. These early experiences instilled in her a resilience and a resourcefulness that would later become hallmarks of her criminal endeavors. But they also sowed the seeds of a darker side, one that would manifest in her later years.

Norwegian folklore and local superstitions played a significant role in Brynhild's upbringing. Tales of trolls lurking in the forests, draugr haunting the sea, and huldra luring men to their doom were common. These stories, rich in dark and mystical elements, likely influenced Brynhild's imagination, painting a world where the line between reality and the supernatural was thin, where the extraordinary was possible. This blend of harsh reality and fantastical storytelling shaped her worldview, adding layers to her complex personality and sparking a curiosity in the audience about the power of storytelling in shaping a person's psyche.

Family dynamics in the Storset household were equally formative. Brynhild's father was a strict and demanding man. He ruled the household with an iron fist, expecting obedience and hard work from his children. This environment of rigid discipline and control may have sparked an early fascination with power in Brynhild. Her mother, on the other hand, played a more subdued role. She was the caretaker, the one who held the fragile family unit together. In this duality, Brynhild saw the contrasting forces of authority and subservience, dominance and submission, a contrast that would shape her future actions.

Berit's quiet endurance often masked a deeper sorrow—one that came from years of submission to her husband's will and the relentless demands of a life spent in survival mode. Her relationship with Brynhild was strained, with little warmth passing between them. Berit's role as the emotional anchor of the family also made her a figure of both pity and disdain in her daughter's eyes. Brynhild observed her mother's endless sacrifices and silently vowed never to live a life of quiet desperation, determined instead to seize control of her destiny, no matter the cost.

Sibling relationships in the Storset family were fraught with tension. Competition for their father's approval and the limited resources available created rivalries. Brynhild, with her strong will and cunning nature, often found herself at odds with her siblings. These early conflicts honed her skills in manipulation and deceit. She learned to navigate the complex web of familial relationships, a skill that would later serve her well in her criminal activities.

The siblings often found themselves pitted against one another, vying for scraps of their father's limited praise and attention. Disagreements over the distribution of food or tasks on the farm frequently erupted into full-blown conflicts, with Brynhild proving particularly adept at turning these disputes to her advantage. Her sharp wit and cunning allowed her to manipulate the family dynamics, ensuring she remained in her father's good graces while quietly fostering resentment among her siblings. These early lessons in control and deceit laid the groundwork for the more sinister manipulations she would later employ.

From a young age, there were signs of troubling behavior. Anecdotes from local community members hinted at a girl who was different, one who exhibited a disturbing lack of empathy. There were whispers of cruelty to animals, a common early indicator of more severe antisocial behavior. Brynhild's interactions with local authorities and community figures were marked by a cunning ability to present a facade of innocence, masking her darker inclinations.

The socio-cultural context of rural Norway during Brynhild's upbringing was one of limited opportunities, especially for women. Educational prospects for girls were scant, often limited to basic literacy and domestic skills. Prevailing gender roles dictated that a woman's place was in the home, her value measured by her ability to maintain a household and raise children. Economic pressures were ever-present, driving many to seek better lives elsewhere. Emigration was a common dream, a beacon of hope for those trapped in the cycle of poverty.

In this environment, Brynhild's ambitions and desires began to take shape. The harsh realities of her childhood, combined with the restrictive societal norms that dictated a woman's place was in the home and her value was measured by her ability to maintain a household and raise children, planted the seeds of her future actions. She yearned for something more, something beyond the confines of her rural upbringing. This yearning, coupled with her innate cunning and manipulative tendencies, set her on a path that would lead to the infamous legacy of Belle Gunness.

As you delve deeper into her story, consider how these early experiences and societal pressures shaped Brynhild's psyche. Reflect on the complex interplay of nature and nurture and how the harsh environment of Selbu, combined with her personal ambitions, sowed the seeds of her notorious future.

FAMILY DYNAMICS AND EARLY INFLUENCES

The Storset household was a microcosm of the strict and often unforgiving world outside. Belle's father, Paul Pedersen Storset, was a man of rigid discipline and unyielding expectations. His stern demeanor and harsh methods of discipline created an atmosphere of fear and obedience. Paul's word was law, and his children learned early on that defiance would not be tolerated. He demanded hard work and absolute compliance, shaping a young Brynhild into someone who understood the power of control and the consequences of crossing authority. This strict upbringing, under a father who demanded absolute compliance, may have planted the seeds for her later need to dominate and manipulate those around her.

In stark contrast, Belle's mother, Berit Olsdatter Storset, embodied compliance and subservience. She fulfilled the traditional role of a Norwegian wife and mother, tending to the household and ensuring her husband's demands were met. Berit's quiet endurance and acceptance of her lot in life provided a model of subservience that Brynhild would internalize but later reject. Instead of adopting her mother's passive acceptance, Brynhild seemed to develop a desire to wield the kind of power her father held. Observing her mother's subjugation may have fueled her determination never to be in a position of weakness or dependence, leading her to reject traditional gender roles.

The dynamics among the Storset siblings were equally complex. Competition for their father's approval was fierce, and favoritism or neglect depended on who best met his expectations. These rivalries created a breeding ground for jealousy and conflict. Brynhild, with her sharp mind and strong will, often found herself both envied and resented by her siblings. These early familial conflicts honed her skills in manipulation and deceit. Learning to navigate the intricate web of sibling alliances and competitions, she developed a keen understanding of how to use others to her advantage—an understanding that would later manifest in her deadly schemes.

Economic pressures were a constant in the Storset household. The family's financial struggles were a daily reminder of the harsh realities of life in rural Norway. The local economy offered little opportunity for advancement, and the Storsets were no exception. The relentless grind of poverty not only shaped Brynhild's early experiences but also fueled her ambitions. The dream of escaping this cycle of hardship was ever-present, and the stories of those who had emigrated to America and found success were a beacon of hope. The economic conditions of her childhood planted the desire for financial security and independence, a desire that later morphed into a ruthless pursuit of wealth through any means necessary.

Early role models and influences in Brynhild's life extended beyond her immediate family. Local authority figures, such as the village priest or community leaders, played significant roles in shaping her worldview. These figures represented power and control, traits that Brynhild seemed to both fear and covet. Additionally, the tales of local criminals or legends provided a different kind of inspiration. Stories of individuals who defied societal norms and achieved infamy fascinated her. The blending of these influences created a complex moral landscape in which Brynhild navigated her formative years.

The influence of folklore and superstitions cannot be understated. The rich tapestry of Norwegian mythology, with its tales of trolls, draugr, and huldra, created a backdrop of mysticism and fear. These stories, with their themes of deception and danger, likely resonated with Brynhild. They painted a world where cunning and ruthlessness were necessary for survival, reinforcing the lessons she learned from her family and community. The intersection of these cultural stories with her personal experiences created a fertile ground for the development of her manipulative and violent tendencies.

In the harsh economic and social landscape of rural Norway, Brynhild's ambitions began to crystallize. The unrelenting poverty, coupled with the rigid societal norms, forged a young woman who was determined to escape her circumstances. The lessons she learned from her parents, the rivalries with her siblings, the influence of local figures, and the rich folklore of her homeland all combined to shape a complex and driven individual. As Brynhild grew older, these influences would guide her actions and decisions, setting her on a path that would eventually lead to the infamous legacy of Belle Gunness.

THE IMMIGRANT DREAM

The decision to leave Norway was not taken lightly by Brynhild Paulsdatter Storset. The dream of America, with its promises of endless opportunities and prosperity, beckoned to many in the grim reality of 19th-century Norway. Belle, like many others, was drawn to the stories of success that filtered back from across the Atlantic. Tales of farmers turning into landowners, laborers becoming entrepreneurs, and impoverished families finding a measure of wealth filled the air, creating a powerful allure. The relentless economic pressures at home, combined with her personal ambitions, made the idea of starting anew in the land of opportunity irresistible.

The journey to America was fraught with challenges. Belle boarded a crowded steamship, embarking on a perilous voyage that would change her life forever. The Atlantic crossing was an ordeal marked by cramped quarters, seasickness, and the ever-present fear of the unknown. As the ship creaked and groaned against the waves, Belle could only imagine what awaited her. The promise of America shone like a beacon, yet the reality of reaching it was daunting. Upon arrival, the bustling port city of New York overwhelmed her senses. The noise, the crowds, the sheer scale of the metropolis was unlike anything she had ever experienced.

From New York, Belle made her way to Chicago, a city teeming with immigrant life. The transition was anything but smooth. Language barriers posed significant challenges, and the cultural adjustments were daunting. The Scandinavian community in Chicago provided some solace, but even within this enclave, survival required cunning and resourcefulness. Finding employment was a struggle, and Belle quickly realized that she needed to adapt or perish. She took on menial jobs, working long hours for meager wages. The harsh realities of her new life tested her resilience but also sharpened her instincts for survival.

Housing was another challenge. The immigrant neighborhoods were crowded and often unsanitary. Belle had to navigate these difficult living conditions while trying to establish herself. The tenements of Chicago were a far cry from the open spaces of rural Norway, but they offered her a foothold in the new world. She quickly learned to build a social network, leveraging connections within the Norwegian community. These early interactions displayed the cunning and manipulative traits that would later define her criminal career. Belle knew how to present herself, how to gain trust, and how to use people to her advantage.

Despite these hardships, Belle's determination never wavered. She secured her first job, working as a maid for a wealthy family. This position provided her with valuable insights into the lives of the affluent, insights that she would later exploit. She observed their habits, their vulnerabilities, and their weaknesses. This knowledge became a part of her growing arsenal of manipulative tactics. She began to understand the power dynamics at play and how she could navigate them to her benefit.

Building a social network was crucial for Belle's survival and success. She ingrained herself within the local Norwegian community, attending social gatherings and church events. Her charm and seemingly genuine demeanor helped her gain the trust of those around her. Yet, beneath this facade, Belle was always calculating, always looking for opportunities to advance her position. She understood the value of connections and used them skillfully to create a web of support and influence.

In these early years, there were subtle indications of Belle's darker inclinations. She displayed an uncanny ability to manipulate those around her, often bending situations to her favor. Her resourcefulness was evident in how she handled the various challenges she faced. These traits, while not overtly sinister at the time, hinted at the lengths she would go to achieve her ambitions. Belle's early experiences in America were a crucible in which her future criminal persona was forged. The immigrant dream, with all its promise and peril, set the stage for the transformation of Brynhild Paulsdatter Storset into Belle Gunness, the notorious femme fatale whose name would become synonymous with terror and deceit.

SETTLING IN AMERICA

Belle Gunness, having left behind her old life in Norway, arrived in America ready to transform herself. The transition required more than just physical relocation; it demanded a complete reinvention of her identity. She adopted the name Belle Petersen, shedding Brynhild Paulsdatter Storset like a snake shedding its skin. This new identity was not just a name change but a declaration of her intent to start anew. Belle altered her appearance to blend into her new surroundings, adopting the dress and mannerisms of American women. She became more outgoing, more charming, and more adept at presenting herself as a respectable member of society. This transformation was the first step in building a new social persona that would enable her to manipulate those around her with ease.

In 1884, Belle married Mads Sorenson, a fellow Norwegian immigrant. Their meeting was fortuitous, perhaps even orchestrated by Belle herself. Mads was drawn to her apparent warmth and industrious nature. Their relationship, however, was far from idyllic. It was marked by Belle's calculated coldness and Mads' unsuspecting trust. The marriage was a union of convenience for Belle, a stepping stone towards greater financial security. Belle convinced Mads to take out multiple life insurance policies, a decision that would later prove fatal for him. She orchestrated a scheme to collect on these policies, ensuring they overlapped in coverage. When Mads died suddenly of a supposed cerebral hemorrhage, Belle collected the insurance money, further securing her financial future. This cunning manipulation set the stage for her future actions, revealing her willingness to use those closest to her as mere pawns in her quest for wealth.

The move to La Porte, Indiana, marked a significant turning point for Belle. La Porte, with its rural setting and tight-knit community, provided the perfect backdrop for her crimes. The decision to relocate was driven by the desire for a fresh start and the opportunity to acquire a larger property. Belle used the insurance money from Mads' death to purchase a farm, a sprawling piece of land that offered both seclusion and opportunity. The acquisition of the farm was strategic; it allowed her to create a façade of respectability while providing the privacy needed to carry out her nefarious activities. Her initial interactions with the La Porte community were calculated, designed to establish her as a hardworking widow and devoted mother. She attended church, participated in local events, and built a network of acquaintances, all while hiding her true intentions.

Early signs of Belle's criminal tendencies began to manifest during her initial years in La Porte. Her first fraudulent activities were relatively small-scale but indicative of her growing ambition. She engaged in minor insurance scams, exaggerating the value of lost or damaged property to collect larger payouts. These early schemes were a testing ground for her more elaborate plans. Belle's interactions with her neighbors and acquaintances were marked by a subtle manipulation. She ingratiated herself with those who could offer her something of value, whether it was information, resources, or unwitting assistance in her schemes. She was adept at reading people, understanding their weaknesses, and exploiting them to her advantage.

As Belle settled into her new life, she began to lay the groundwork for her future crimes. The farm in La Porte became the staging ground for a series of murders that would shock the world. She placed personal ads in Norwegian-language newspapers, targeting wealthy men who were seeking companionship. These men, lured by the promise of love and prosperity, visited the farm, never to be seen again. Belle's manipulative charm and calculated deceit allowed her to gain their trust before murdering them and disposing of their bodies. Each victim was carefully chosen, their wealth and social isolation making them ideal targets. Belle's ability to manipulate public perception and hide in plain sight enabled her to continue her murderous activities for years without arousing suspicion.

The societal and forensic limitations of the early 20th century played a crucial role in Belle's ability to evade capture. The science of criminal investigation was rudimentary, with limited tools and techniques available to law enforcement. This lack of sophistication allowed Belle to operate under the radar, her crimes hidden beneath a veneer of respectability. The close-knit nature of the La Porte community, coupled with Belle's carefully crafted persona, made it difficult for authorities to see her for what she truly was.

Exploring Belle Gunness's case through a historical and psychological lens reveals the complexities of her character and the societal factors that enabled her crimes. It offers valuable insights into early forensic science, gender roles, and the psychology of a woman who defied societal norms to become one of America's most notorious serial killers. Readers will find themselves drawn into a story of shock, empathy, and reflection, questioning how societal pressures and personal ambitions can shape a criminal mind. Belle's story is not just a tale of murder and deceit; it is a window into the darker aspects of human nature and the societal conditions that allow them to flourish.

As we move forward, we will delve deeper into the life and mind of Belle Gunness, piecing together the events that led to her infamy and exploring the lasting impact of her crimes on society.

CHAPTER 2

THE MAKING OF A MURDERER

The bustling streets of Chicago were a far cry from the serene yet harsh landscapes of rural Norway. When Belle Gunness, then known as Brynhild Paulsdatter Storset, arrived in the city in 1881, she was thrust into a world of rapid industrialization and burgeoning immigrant communities. Chicago, with its smokestacks and crowded tenements, was both a land of opportunity and a place of great struggle. For Belle, it was the perfect setting to reinvent herself and lay the groundwork for her future misdeeds.

LIFE IN CHICAGO

Settling in the heart of Chicago's Norwegian immigrant community, Belle found herself in an area known for its tight-knit social fabric and shared cultural heritage. She first took residence in the neighborhoods north of the Chicago River, which were densely populated with fellow Norwegians. These neighborhoods, though vibrant with life, were often plagued by poverty and cramped living conditions. Belle, like many others, found work as a maid and later in a factory, jobs that were typical for women of her background. The wages were meager, barely enough to scrape by, but they provided her a foothold in this new world.

Within the Norwegian enclave, Belle quickly learned the value of connections. She attended church regularly, not out of religious fervor, but as a means to network. She ingratiated herself with key figures in the community, building relationships that would later prove advantageous. These early days in Chicago were a mix of hard work and strategic social maneuvering. Belle's ability to navigate this immigrant network with charm and cunning was the first indication of her manipulative prowess.

While Belle outwardly conformed to the expectations of the immigrant community, she privately harbored more ambitious plans. She quickly identified those who could provide her with financial support or valuable connections, ingratiating herself with the right people. At church functions and community events, she would often recount exaggerated tales of her struggles, carefully playing the role of the hard-luck immigrant trying to make her way in the New World. Behind her sympathetic façade, however, she was constantly scheming, calculating how to turn these relationships to her advantage. These early manipulations were a precursor to the far more dangerous deceptions she would later craft.

Financially, Belle was always scheming for a way out of the grinding poverty that characterized her early years in America. The low wages she earned as a domestic worker were insufficient for her ambitions. She aspired to wealth and social status, dreaming of a life far removed from the one she had known in Norway. To achieve this, she employed various strategies to save and invest money. Belle was not above deceit; she was known to exaggerate her financial struggles to elicit sympathy and financial aid from her acquaintances. This early penchant for manipulation hinted at the more sinister tactics she would later employ.

Belle's social network in Chicago was a carefully curated blend of friendships and alliances. She formed key relationships with influential members of the Norwegian community, individuals who could offer her support and resources. Her relationships with men were particularly telling. Belle had a way of presenting herself as a desirable partner, often leading men to believe she was genuinely interested in them. In reality, she viewed these relationships as transactions, opportunities to further her own goals. This early manipulation of romantic interests was a precursor to the matrimonial schemes she would later orchestrate with deadly precision.

Even in these early days, there were signs of Belle's deceptive nature. She was involved in minor fraudulent activities, such as inflating the value of lost or stolen property to collect larger insurance payouts. This willingness to engage in deceitful practices was not lost on those around her. Anecdotes from acquaintances paint a picture of a woman who could be both charming and ruthless, depending on what the situation demanded. Employers and landlords often found themselves on the receiving end of her manipulative tactics, whether it was through sob stories designed to delay rent payments or cunning ploys to secure better working conditions.

Belle's early life in Chicago was a crucible in which her darker tendencies were forged. The city, with its mix of opportunity and hardship, provided the perfect backdrop for her transformation. It was here that she honed her skills in manipulation, deceit, and social navigation. These early experiences laid the foundation for the more heinous crimes she would commit later in life. Belle Gunness was not just made by her actions but by the environment that shaped her, an environment where survival often meant bending the rules and exploiting every opportunity.

As you continue to explore Belle's story, consider how her early life in Chicago, with its blend of struggle and ambition, influenced her path. Reflect on the ways in which her interactions, both genuine and deceptive, shaped her into the notorious figure she would become. The city's bustling streets and crowded tenements were the training grounds for a woman who would go on to become one of America's most infamous female serial killers.

THE FIRST MARRIAGE: MADS SORENSON

Belle Gunness's life in Chicago took a pivotal turn when she met Mads Sorenson, a fellow Norwegian immigrant. Their introduction came through mutual acquaintances within the tight-knit Norwegian community. Belle, with her striking presence and determined demeanor, quickly caught Mads's eye. The initial attraction was mutual, and their courtship progressed swiftly. Belle presented herself as a hardworking and devoted woman, qualities that resonated with Mads. Their relationship blossomed against the backdrop of Chicago's bustling immigrant neighborhoods, culminating in a modest yet joyful wedding ceremony in 1884. Friends and family gathered to celebrate, unaware of the dark future that lay ahead.

The dynamics within Belle and Mads's marriage were complex and, at times, unsettling. Belle, ever the calculating individual, managed to wield significant influence over Mads. She was the driving force behind many of their decisions, particularly those involving finances. The couple shared common goals of financial stability and upward mobility, but it was Belle who often took the lead in their pursuit. Mads, perhaps blinded by love or simply trusting his wife's judgment, acquiesced to Belle's plans without much resistance. This power imbalance allowed Belle to steer the course of their marriage, setting the stage for the manipulative schemes that would follow.

Belle's influence over Mads extended beyond their day-to-day decisions. She manipulated him into taking out life insurance policies under the guise of protecting their future. To outsiders, her insistence on these policies seemed like a prudent, even loving, act of a concerned wife. Yet, her true intentions were far darker. The overlapping policies provided the perfect opportunity for Belle to orchestrate a murder that would appear as a natural death. She understood the financial system and the loopholes it offered, allowing her to devise a plan that would enrich her at the expense of her unsuspecting husband. This level of premeditation demonstrated just how cold and calculated Belle had become.

One of the most telling aspects of their marriage was the life insurance policies taken out on Mads Sorenson. Belle, with her keen eye for financial opportunities, convinced Mads to secure multiple policies. These policies, each with substantial payouts, overlapped in their coverage. Belle's role in this decision was pivotal; she persuaded Mads of the necessity for such security, framing it as a prudent step for their future. The insurance companies involved in these policies were reputable, yet they became unwitting participants in Belle's sinister plans. The overlapping terms of the policies meant that there was a brief window during which Mads was covered by both, a detail that would later prove crucial.

Mads Sorenson's death on July 30, 1900, was shrouded in suspicion. Officially, the cause of death was listed as heart failure, a diagnosis that conveniently aligned with the symptoms of poisoning. Belle's behavior following Mads's death was notably composed, even as she made the necessary arrangements to collect the insurance payouts. Her calm demeanor raised eyebrows, but no concrete evidence linked her to foul play. The community and Mads's family were understandably shocked by his sudden passing. Whispers of doubt and suspicion circulated, but Belle's outward display of grief and her status as a grieving widow helped to quell most of the immediate concerns.

The aftermath of Mads Sorenson's death saw Belle receiving significant payouts from the overlapping insurance policies. These funds, meant to provide security in the event of a tragedy, instead became the foundation upon which Belle would build her next chapter. The substantial financial windfall allowed her to make immediate decisions that furthered her ambitions. She invested in property and other ventures, always with an eye towards increasing her wealth and securing her future. The community's reactions to her newfound wealth were mixed. Some offered congratulations, believing Belle to be a prudent and fortunate widow. Others, however, harbored suspicions, their doubts fueled by the seemingly fortuitous timing of Mads's death.

Belle's ability to maintain a respectable facade in the wake of such a significant loss was a testament to her manipulative skills. She continued to foster relationships within the Norwegian community, presenting herself as a model of resilience and determination. Yet, beneath this veneer, Belle's mind was always working, always plotting the next move. The financial security provided by the insurance payouts emboldened her, setting the stage for the even more audacious schemes that would follow.

As you delve deeper into the life of Belle Gunness, consider the intricate web of manipulation and deceit she wove around those closest to her. Reflect on how her early experiences and relationships shaped her into a figure capable of such calculated and cold-blooded actions. The story of Belle and Mads Sorenson is not just one of marital union but of a deadly partnership where one spouse's trust became the other's lethal weapon.

THE INSURANCE PAYOUT

The death of Mads Sorenson and the subsequent insurance payouts marked a turning point in Belle Gunness's life. The sums she received were substantial, reflecting her meticulous planning. From the overlapping policies, Belle collected a total of $8,500, a significant amount of money in the early 1900s. This financial windfall provided her with the means to transform her life and pursue her ambitious plans. She wasted no time in making immediate financial decisions. Belle used part of the money to settle outstanding debts, ensuring her financial slate was clean. She then invested a portion in various ventures, primarily focused on securing long-term stability and wealth. One of her first major purchases was property, which laid the groundwork for her next phase of operations.

The reactions from those around Belle to her sudden wealth were mixed. Family members and close friends were divided; some congratulated her on her newfound fortune, while others harbored deep suspicions. The circumstances surrounding Mads's death were too convenient for many to ignore. Whispers of foul play circulated within her social circles, but Belle's composed demeanor and strategic interactions helped maintain a respectable facade. Public perception varied; some saw her as a shrewd and resilient widow, while others were less convinced by her display of grief. Local gossip painted a picture of a woman who was either incredibly fortunate or disturbingly cunning. Belle's efforts to maintain her image were relentless. She participated in community events, donated to local causes, and continued to present herself as a devoted mother and widow, all while secretly planning her next moves.

Belle's financial cunning didn't end with the insurance money from Mads's death. She continued to engage in various schemes to increase her wealth. One of her strategies involved taking out additional insurance policies on other individuals, often without their knowledge. These policies served as a safety net, ensuring that Belle would benefit financially from any future "accidents." She also explored business ventures, using the payout money to invest in small businesses and real estate. These investments were carefully chosen to maximize returns while minimizing risk. Belle's fraudulent activities continued in parallel. She manipulated financial records, exaggerated losses, and even staged minor accidents to collect on insurance claims. Her ability to weave a web of deception was unparalleled, allowing her to amass a considerable fortune without arousing significant suspicion.

The insurance payout from Mads's death was not just a financial boon; it was a catalyst for Belle's evolving criminal mindset. With a substantial amount of money at her disposal, she began to plan for a more ambitious future. The search for a new property became a priority. Belle wanted a location that offered both seclusion and the potential for further financial gain. Her sights eventually settled on La Porte, Indiana, a rural area that promised a fresh start and ample opportunities for her schemes. The decision to move was strategic. La Porte's rural setting provided the privacy she needed to carry out her plans without the constant scrutiny of urban life. The move was meticulously planned, with Belle preparing every detail to ensure a smooth transition. She liquidated assets in Chicago, secured transportation for her belongings, and even made arrangements for her foster children.

Belle's ambitions grew with her newfound wealth. The money allowed her to think bigger, to plan more elaborate schemes that required significant resources. She envisioned a life where financial security was guaranteed, no matter the cost. This evolving mindset was marked by an increasing ruthlessness. Belle was no longer content with small-scale fraud; she aimed for larger, more profitable ventures. Her criminal activities became more sophisticated, involving complex financial manipulations and carefully staged events. The move to La Porte was just the beginning, a stepping stone towards a future where Belle Gunness would become one of America's most infamous female serial killers.

THE MOVE TO LA PORTE, INDIANA

Belle Gunness's decision to leave Chicago behind was driven by a desire for a fresh start and the allure of a larger property. The bustling city had served its purpose, providing the initial financial gains and social networks she needed. But Belle yearned for more—a place where she could operate with greater freedom and less scrutiny. La Porte, Indiana, with its rural charm and expanding opportunities, seemed the perfect destination. The rural life offered the seclusion she craved, away from the prying eyes of urban neighbors. Additionally, La Porte's growing community promised new opportunities for financial and social advancement. Belle had likely heard of La Porte through acquaintances or during prior visits, and she sensed the potential it held for her ambitious plans.

Acquiring the farm in La Porte was a meticulously planned endeavor. The property itself was expansive, featuring a large farmhouse, several outbuildings, and ample land that stretched far enough to ensure privacy. The financial transactions involved in the purchase were straightforward, thanks to the funds Belle had amassed from her previous schemes. She interacted with local real estate agents and the seller with the same charm and composure that had served her so well in Chicago. The seller, unaware of Belle's sinister intentions, saw her as a respectable widow looking to start anew in the countryside. The farm's features, including its isolation and the fertile soil, made it ideal for both legitimate farming and more nefarious activities.

Integrating into the La Porte community required a careful balancing act. Belle's first interactions with her new neighbors were marked by her characteristic charm and friendliness. She presented herself as a hardworking widow devoted to her children and her farm. Belle attended church regularly, participated in community events, and made an effort to befriend her neighbors. Her presence at social gatherings and local functions helped to solidify her image as a respectable member of the community. This facade was essential for her plans; it allowed her to build trust and deflect any potential suspicions about her activities. Belle's ability to seamlessly insert herself into the social fabric of La Porte was a testament to her manipulative skills.

The move to La Porte set the stage for Belle's future crimes in several ways. One of her first actions upon settling in was to make renovations and changes to the farm. These modifications were not merely for comfort but were strategic adjustments to facilitate her criminal activities. She established secluded areas for disposing of bodies and created spaces within the house that allowed for easy control and confinement of her victims. Belle's initial steps in her criminal plans involved placing personal ads in Norwegian-language newspapers, targeting wealthy men seeking companionship. These ads were crafted to lure potential victims to her farm, where they would fall prey to her deadly schemes.

The careful construction of these personal ads reflected Belle's understanding of human desire. She knew how to appeal to the loneliness and vulnerability of men searching for companionship. Her letters were crafted with just the right blend of warmth and business-like practicality, offering the promise of a stable, prosperous life on her farm. Once she had ensnared their interest, Belle reeled them in with promises of shared wealth and a future together. These men, blinded by the hope of love and prosperity, rarely realized the trap they were walking into until it was too late. Belle's ability to play on human emotions was key to her success as a predator.

Building relationships with potential victims was an integral part of Belle's strategy. She corresponded with her targets through letters, building trust and rapport before inviting them to La Porte. Once there, Belle's charm and the promise of a prosperous life together disarmed any suspicions they might have had. These men, often isolated from their own communities and captivated by Belle's apparent warmth, were easy prey. Belle's ability to manipulate these relationships, combined with the privacy afforded by her farm, allowed her to carry out her crimes with chilling efficiency.

Belle Gunness's move to La Porte, Indiana, was more than a change of scenery; it was a calculated step in her evolving criminal enterprise. The combination of rural seclusion, a supportive community, and her own cunning set the stage for a series of murders that would shock the nation. As you explore Belle's life in La Porte, consider how this new environment enabled her to refine and expand her deadly operations. Reflect on the ways in which her interactions with the community and her potential victims reveal the depths of her manipulative nature. Belle's story in La Porte is a testament to her ability to adapt and thrive, even as her actions grew increasingly sinister.

CHAPTER 3
THE MURDER FARM

The morning fog rolled over the fields of La Porte, Indiana, as Belle Gunness set her sights on a new chapter in her life. Her aspirations were cloaked under the guise of a fresh start, but the true horror of her intentions lay hidden beneath her seemingly innocent plans. La Porte, with its fertile lands and welcoming community, seemed an ideal place for Belle to weave her dark web. The farm she acquired would soon become infamous, a place where dreams turned into nightmares.

ACQUIRING THE FARM

Belle Gunness approached the purchase of her new farm with the same meticulous planning that characterized her previous endeavors. The process began with careful scouting and selection. She sought a property that offered both seclusion and the potential for financial gain. After identifying a suitable farm, Belle entered negotiations with the seller. The purchase price was set at $3,000—a substantial amount at the time, but well within Belle's reach due to the insurance payouts she had previously secured. Her interactions with real estate agents were marked by a blend of charm and shrewdness. Belle presented herself as a hardworking widow, eager to start anew. Her negotiation tactics were calculated, ensuring she secured favorable terms while maintaining the illusion of a genuine and earnest buyer.

The property itself was expansive, featuring a large farmhouse, several outbuildings, and ample land. The layout of the farm provided the privacy Belle needed for her sinister plans. The farmhouse was robust, with multiple rooms that could be easily adapted for various purposes. The barns and outbuildings offered additional spaces for storage and concealment. The land stretched far, bordered by dense woods that provided a natural barrier from prying eyes. For Belle, this was not just a home; it was a carefully chosen stage for her criminal activities.

Upon acquiring the farm, Belle wasted no time in making the necessary renovations to suit her needs. The house underwent significant modifications. Rooms were rearranged and repurposed to facilitate easy cleanup after murders. Heavy furniture was strategically placed to create hiding spots and to block off areas where bodies could be temporarily stored. The barns were similarly adapted. Belle installed hidden compartments and traps to ensure that any evidence of her crimes could be quickly concealed. Landscaping changes were also made. Shrubs and trees were planted strategically to obscure views of certain areas of the property. Paths were created to allow for discreet movement around the farm, ensuring Belle could transport bodies without being seen.

Every adjustment Belle made was calculated with chilling precision. The heavy furniture, chosen for its durability, could easily be used to block off sections of the house if needed, keeping unwanted eyes from discovering her secrets. She also ensured that certain areas, like the basement, were outfitted with tools for dismemberment and quicklime for hastening decomposition. This level of foresight in modifying her surroundings demonstrated just how methodical Belle had become in planning not just for the murders but also for the aftermath, where evidence needed to be erased swiftly and efficiently.

Setting up the farm for her criminal activities required meticulous planning and execution. Belle structured her home to create distinct areas for different stages of her murderous process. The farmhouse had areas designated for victim interaction—rooms that were warm and inviting, designed to put her targets at ease. These spaces were furnished comfortably, with personal touches that reinforced Belle's facade of a caring and nurturing widow. In stark contrast, other parts of the house and outbuildings were designated for the gruesome tasks of murder and body disposal. These areas were stark, functional, and easy to clean. Belle ensured that tools and materials needed for her crimes were always within reach, yet hidden from casual view.

The logistics of maintaining her criminal operations were complex. Belle employed specific tactics to avoid raising suspicion in the community. She was careful to stagger the arrivals of her victims, ensuring that no one noticed a sudden influx of strangers to her farm. Bodies were disposed of methodically, often buried in different locations to avoid creating obvious gravesites. Quicklime was used to hasten decomposition, reducing the chances of discovery. Belle also maintained a rigorous schedule for her farm activities, blending mundane tasks with her criminal endeavors. This routine helped to create a sense of normalcy, deflecting any potential curiosity from neighbors or local authorities.

Integrating into the La Porte community was crucial for Belle's plans. She understood that maintaining a respectable image would allow her to carry out her crimes with minimal suspicion. Belle attended church regularly, participating in social events and gatherings. Her presence at these functions helped to reinforce her image as a devoted widow and mother. She built relationships with her neighbors, often inviting them over for meals or offering help with their own farm work. Belle's generosity extended to volunteering and charitable activities. She donated to local causes and offered assistance to those in need, further solidifying her standing in the community.

Belle's charm was her greatest asset in maintaining her double life. Her neighbors saw her as generous and kind-hearted, always willing to lend a hand or offer advice. She frequently hosted dinners, where she would present herself as the perfect hostess, radiating warmth and hospitality. These gatherings served as both a way to solidify her standing in the community and a strategic move to divert suspicion. By embedding herself so deeply within the social fabric of La Porte, Belle ensured that any whispers of foul play would seem outlandish, easily dismissed by those who had broken bread at her table.

Belle's ability to present herself as a pillar of the community was a key element in her success. Her neighbors saw her as a hardworking, compassionate woman dedicated to her family and her farm. This carefully crafted persona allowed her to operate under the radar, masking the true nature of her activities. The trust and goodwill she garnered from her community provided a shield, deflecting any potential scrutiny.

In La Porte, Belle Gunness found the perfect environment to continue her deadly pursuits. The farm, with its strategic layout and modifications, became the stage for a series of crimes that would shock the nation. Her ability to blend into the community, coupled with her meticulous planning, allowed her to carry out her sinister plans with chilling efficiency. As you uncover the details of Belle's life on the Murder Farm, consider the intricate balance she maintained between her public persona and her secret life. Reflect on how her interactions with her neighbors and her strategic modifications to the farm reveal the depths of her cunning and the lengths she would go to achieve her dark ambitions.

THE FIRST VICTIMS

Belle Gunness meticulously selected her first victims, focusing on wealthy, single men who were often isolated from their families. The criteria were simple but effective. She targeted men who had substantial financial resources but lacked close ties that might prompt immediate and thorough investigations if they went missing. Belle's methods of contacting these men were equally calculated. She placed personal ads in newspapers, particularly those read by Norwegian immigrants. These ads, promising companionship and a prosperous future, were crafted to appeal to lonely, affluent men seeking a fresh start.

The initial interactions were designed to build trust. Belle corresponded with her targets through letters, painting a picture of a warm and inviting home. She often included photographs of herself and the farm, showcasing a life of potential happiness. The invitations to visit her farm were both enticing and reassuring, promising a genuine opportunity for love and prosperity. These men, drawn by Belle's charm and the prospect of a new beginning, were easily lured into her deadly trap.

Belle was a master at constructing an image of herself that her suitors found irresistible. Her letters were filled with details of the farm's bounty, the potential for partnership, and the promise of a loving, comfortable life. She knew exactly how to frame her words to create an emotional connection, presenting herself as not only a potential wife but also a business partner, someone who could help them realize their dreams. This mixture of romance and practicality made her offers nearly impossible to refuse, especially for men who were already isolated from their families and looking for a fresh start.

The first known victims of Belle Gunness were John Moe and Ole B. Budsberg. John Moe, a recent arrival from Minnesota, was enchanted by Belle's letters and her promises of a prosperous future together. Upon his arrival at the farm, Belle greeted him warmly, but the hospitality was short-lived. Belle poisoned John, watching as the life slowly drained from his body. Once he was dead, she disposed of his body by burying it in a shallow grave on her property. Ole B. Budsberg, an elderly widower from Wisconsin, met a similar fate. Belle bludgeoned him, ensuring his death was swift. His body was also buried on the farm, concealed beneath layers of soil and secrecy.

Belle's methods of murder were diverse and meticulously planned. She used poison, often strychnine, to incapacitate her victims. In some cases, she resorted to blunt force, using heavy objects to deliver fatal blows. The disposal of the bodies was equally calculated. She buried many of them on her property, choosing locations that were unlikely to be disturbed. In other instances, she burned the remains, reducing them to ashes that could be scattered or concealed. These techniques ensured that the evidence of her crimes was effectively erased.

Covering her tracks required a combination of cunning and manipulation. Belle was meticulous in her efforts to erase evidence. She cleaned the crime scenes thoroughly, ensuring no trace of her victims remained. Any personal belongings were either destroyed or hidden away. Belle also took precautions to manipulate local authorities and community members. She cultivated relationships with key figures, ensuring their trust and deflecting any potential suspicions. When inquiries arose from the families of her victims, Belle used fake letters and correspondence to mislead them, creating the illusion that their loved ones had moved on to other places.

The initial impact of the disappearances on the local community was subtle but gradually grew more pronounced. Neighbors and authorities began to notice the pattern of men arriving at the farm and never being seen again. Early suspicions were often dismissed, thanks to Belle's carefully maintained facade. She responded to inquiries with plausible explanations, claiming that the men had left of their own accord. Her reputation as a respectable widow and mother helped to quell any immediate concerns. However, as the number of disappearances increased, whispers of doubt began to circulate within the community.

Authorities conducted initial investigations and missing person reports, but Belle's manipulative tactics often stymied these efforts. She provided misleading information, feigned ignorance, and used her charm to deflect suspicion. The lack of advanced forensic techniques at the time further complicated the investigations. Without concrete evidence, authorities found it difficult to build a case against Belle. Her ability to manipulate public perception and her strategic interactions with the community allowed her to continue her deadly activities with minimal interference.

THE ROLE OF PERSONAL ADS

Belle Gunness employed personal ads as a strategic and insidious tool to lure her victims. The content of these ads was carefully crafted to appeal to lonely, wealthy men seeking companionship and a fresh start. Phrases such as "a comely widow with a large farm" and "seeking a partner for prosperous future" painted a picture of an idyllic life waiting for the right man. These ads promised not just love but also a slice of the American Dream—a prosperous life on a sprawling farm. Belle placed these ads in newspapers popular among Norwegian immigrants, such as the "Skandinaven" and the "Norske Tidende," ensuring they reached a broad audience. The geographic reach of these publications extended beyond Indiana, drawing potential victims from various states.

The process of correspondence and courtship that followed was meticulous. Belle's initial letters were warm and inviting, filled with promises of a happy future together. She often included details about her farm, her children, and the life she envisioned with her new partner. These letters were designed to build trust and create an emotional connection. Belle's writing was persuasive, filled with flattery and assurances that resonated with her targets' desires for companionship and security. As the correspondence continued, she would weave in promises of marriage and shared wealth, painting a picture of a life that was both financially secure and emotionally fulfilling. This gradual build-up of trust and rapport was crucial in convincing these men to leave their homes and travel to La Porte.

Belle's manipulative tactics were sophisticated and psychologically astute. She employed a blend of flattery and emotional manipulation to ensnare her victims. She praised their virtues, expressed admiration for their achievements, and offered empathy for their past hardships. By doing so, she created an emotional bond that made her targets feel valued and understood. Belle exploited their dreams and desires, promising a life that aligned perfectly with their hopes for the future. She often created a sense of urgency or desperation, suggesting that opportunities were fleeting and that they needed to act quickly to secure their happiness. This psychological manipulation was highly effective, preying on the vulnerabilities and aspirations of her targets.

The effectiveness of Belle's personal ad strategy is evident in the number of victims she lured to her farm. By some estimates, she attracted over a dozen men through these ads; each convinced that they were embarking on a new and prosperous chapter of their lives. Belle's ability to execute her plans with such efficiency relied on her meticulous preparation and the emotional groundwork laid through her correspondence. Once her victims arrived, they were often caught in a well-orchestrated trap with minimal suspicion or resistance. The seamless transition from courtship to entrapment allowed Belle to continue her killing spree with alarming success. The trust she built through her letters disarmed her victims, making them easy prey for her lethal intentions. This strategy of using personal ads was not just a means to an end but a testament to Belle's cunning and manipulative prowess.

The personal ads Belle Gunness placed were more than just words on paper; they were the bait in a deadly trap. Each ad was crafted with precision, designed to lure in men who were lonely, wealthy, and seeking a new beginning. The geographic reach of these ads ensured a steady stream of potential victims drawn to the promise of love and prosperity. The letters that followed were equally strategic, building trust and creating an emotional bond that made her targets feel they had found a genuine partner. Belle's psychological manipulation, from flattery to creating a sense of urgency, played on the deepest desires and vulnerabilities of her victims. This method allowed her to continue her murderous activities with chilling efficiency, demonstrating the dark genius behind her strategy. As you consider Belle's use of personal ads, reflect on the power of manipulation and the lengths to which she went to ensnare her victims, turning their dreams of a new life into a fatal nightmare.

THE DISAPPEARANCE OF SUITORS

When each suitor arrived at Belle Gunness's farm, they were greeted with warmth and hospitality. Belle's charm was evident from the moment they set foot on the property. She would often meet them at the train station, her demeanor inviting and reassuring. As they approached the farmhouse, Belle painted a vivid picture of the life they would share together—a prosperous, peaceful existence on a sprawling farm. Her home was meticulously maintained, with cozy furnishings and a welcoming atmosphere. This initial hospitality was designed to put her suitors at ease, making them feel valued and hopeful about their future.

Belle's promises of a shared future were both enticing and manipulative. She spoke of marriage, children, and the joys of farm life. She assured her suitors that their combined efforts would lead to great success. For a brief period, she allowed them to experience this idyllic life. They would help with farm chores, share meals, and even attend local social events as a couple. This period of cohabitation was crucial in solidifying their trust and commitment. Belle's ability to create a convincing facade of normalcy was a key element in her deadly scheme. The suitors, believing they had found true love, were unaware of the fate that awaited them.

The execution of the murders followed a grim and calculated pattern. Belle employed various methods to end the lives of her suitors, each chosen for its effectiveness and minimal risk of detection. Poisoning was a common method. Belle often used strychnine, a potent toxin that caused a slow and agonizing death. She would mix it into food or drink, ensuring her victims ingested a lethal dose. The timing of the murders was strategic. Belle preferred to carry out her deadly acts at night, under the cover of darkness. This reduced the chances of interruption and allowed her to dispose of the bodies without arousing suspicion. In some cases, she resorted to blunt force, using heavy objects to deliver fatal blows. These killings were marked by a cold efficiency, with Belle showing no hesitation or remorse.

Belle's disposal techniques were equally methodical. She buried many of her victims in various locations on the farm. The burial sites were carefully chosen to avoid detection. Some bodies were placed under the hog pen, where the animals would help to obscure any evidence. Quicklime was used to hasten decomposition, ensuring that the remains would deteriorate rapidly. In other instances, Belle burned the bodies, reducing them to ashes that could be scattered or concealed. These techniques ensured that the physical evidence of her crimes was effectively erased. Belle's knowledge of decomposition and her ability to manipulate the environment around her were crucial in maintaining her deadly operations.

Covering up the disappearances required a blend of deception and manipulation. Belle was adept at crafting fake letters and correspondence to mislead the families of her victims. She would write letters in the victim's name, claiming they had moved on to other destinations or found new opportunities. These letters were designed to allay any fears and prevent further inquiries. Belle also manipulated local authorities and community members to avoid suspicion. She maintained her image as a respectable widow, using her charm to deflect any potential concerns. When questioned, she provided plausible explanations for the disappearances, often claiming that her suitors had left voluntarily. Her ability to weave a web of lies and maintain her facade of innocence was a testament to her manipulative prowess.

The disappearances of Belle's suitors cast a dark shadow over the community of La Porte. Neighbors and authorities began to notice the pattern of men arriving at the farm and never being seen again. Early suspicions were often dismissed, thanks to Belle's carefully maintained facade. She responded to inquiries with plausible explanations, claiming that the men had left of their own accord. Her reputation as a respectable widow and mother helped to quell any immediate concerns. However, as the number of disappearances increased, whispers of doubt began to circulate within the community. Authorities conducted initial investigations and missing person reports, but Belle's manipulative tactics often stymied these efforts. She provided misleading information, feigned ignorance, and used her charm to deflect suspicion. The lack of advanced forensic techniques at the time further complicated the investigations. Without concrete evidence, authorities found it difficult to build a case against Belle. Her ability to manipulate public perception and her strategic interactions with the community allowed her to continue her deadly activities with minimal interference.

As Belle Gunness's dark deeds unfolded, the community of La Porte was left grappling with a growing sense of unease. The disappearances of suitors, coupled with Belle's ability to cover her tracks, created an atmosphere of suspicion and fear. The true extent of her crimes would only be revealed much later, leaving a lasting impact on those who had unwittingly become part of her deadly game.

In the next chapter, we will delve deeper into the forensic challenges of the early 20th century and how they played a role in Belle's ability to evade capture.

CHAPTER 4
METHODS OF MURDER

The dawn light was just beginning to illuminate the grim farmstead of Belle Gunness. It was a place where the promise of new beginnings was overshadowed by a dark reality. Here, in this seemingly quaint rural setting, Belle perfected her methods of murder with chilling precision. Her farm in La Porte, Indiana, was not just a home but a well-oiled machine of death. For those who answered her personal ads, it was a one-way ticket to oblivion.

POISONING TECHNIQUES

Belle Gunness's primary choice of weapon was poison, a method that allowed her to kill with a degree of detachment and precision. Two poisons became her tools of choice: arsenic and strychnine. Arsenic, often referred to as the "inheritance powder," was easily accessible during the late 19th and early 20th centuries. Belle likely obtained it from common household items such as rat poison, which was readily available in general stores. Arsenic poisoning was insidious, its symptoms often mistaken for natural illnesses, making it an ideal choice for someone looking to avoid suspicion.

Strychnine was another poison in Belle's deadly arsenal. Its effects were more dramatic and immediate. Strychnine was typically used as a pesticide, and Belle could have acquired it through similar means as arsenic. The symptoms of strychnine poisoning were unmistakable: severe muscle spasms, convulsions, and eventually respiratory failure. The poison acted fast, ensuring that Belle's victims did not suffer long but suffered intensely. This poison left little room for doubt about its deadly nature, yet Belle managed to mask its use effectively.

Belle's methods of administering poison were as varied as they were effective. She often laced food and beverages with the lethal substances. Meals prepared with loving care became the instruments of death. Belle's victims, unaware of the danger, consumed the tainted food and drink, sealing their fate with each bite and sip. The dosages she administered varied. For some, she opted for a gradual approach, adding small amounts of poison over time to mimic the symptoms of a lingering illness. This method allowed her to avoid immediate suspicion as the victims' health deteriorated slowly. For others, Belle used a more immediate approach, delivering a lethal dose in a single serving. This ensured quick and decisive results, minimizing the risk of intervention.

Concealing the taste and effects of the poison required cunning. Arsenic, in small doses, has a slightly metallic taste, but it can be masked by strong flavors or sweeteners. Belle's culinary skills came into play here, allowing her to prepare dishes that effectively disguised the presence of poison. Strychnine, more bitter and harder to conceal, was often used in drinks where its taste could be masked by alcohol or strong flavors. Belle's ability to manipulate the sensory experience of her victims ensured that they consumed the poison without suspicion.

The symptoms experienced by Belle's victims varied depending on the poison used. Initial symptoms of arsenic poisoning included nausea, vomiting, and abdominal cramps. These were easily mistaken for common ailments such as food poisoning or stomach flu. As the poisoning progressed, more severe symptoms like dehydration, shock, and multi-organ failure emerged. Strychnine poisoning, on the other hand, presented more violently. Victims experienced intense muscle spasms and convulsions, progressing to severe seizures and, eventually, respiratory paralysis. The rapid onset of these symptoms left little time for medical intervention, ensuring the poison's effectiveness.

Belle's ability to explain away these symptoms further aided her in avoiding suspicion. She often claimed her victims were suffering from illnesses or accidents. In cases of arsenic poisoning, she might suggest that the victim had contracted a severe stomach bug or had eaten something that disagreed with them. For strychnine poisoning, the dramatic symptoms could be attributed to sudden medical conditions such as seizures or strokes. Belle's calm demeanor and her role as a caring widow helped to reinforce these explanations, deflecting any immediate concerns from friends or relatives.

Covering up the use of poison in her murders required a blend of manipulation and strategic planning. Belle was adept at influencing the opinions of local doctors and authorities. She would often accompany victims to medical appointments, guiding the narrative towards natural causes of illness. Her ability to feign concern and provide plausible explanations ensured that death certificates often listed natural causes rather than foul play. Quick burials were another tactic Belle employed to avoid autopsies. She would expedite the funeral arrangements, often claiming the need for a swift burial due to religious or cultural reasons. This prevented any thorough examination of the bodies, ensuring the true cause of death remained concealed.

Belle's manipulation extended to medical professionals, who, due to the limited forensic knowledge of the time, were easily swayed by her calm demeanor and detailed accounts of her victims' supposed illnesses. In a world where sudden deaths were often attributed to common ailments, Belle thrived in a system ill-equipped to identify subtle foul play. Her meticulous record-keeping of her victims' 'symptoms' provided doctors with a convincing backstory, reducing the likelihood of any autopsy being ordered.

Discrediting suspicions from friends or relatives was another key aspect of Belle's strategy. She maintained a network of trust within the community, leveraging her reputation as a respectable widow to deflect any doubts. When questioned about the sudden illness of a suitor or a child, Belle would provide detailed, plausible accounts of their declining health. She often involved multiple community members in these narratives, ensuring a consistent story that was hard to dispute. Any persistent concerns were met with calculated empathy and reassurances, effectively neutralizing potential threats to her deadly activities.

As you delve deeper into the methods of Belle Gunness, consider the meticulous planning and cold calculation that defined her use of poison. Reflect on how her ability to manipulate not only her victims but also the community around her allowed her to carry out her crimes with such chilling efficiency. The farm in La Porte was not just a place of death but a testament to Belle's dark ingenuity and her mastery of the art of murder.

THE USE OF BLUNT FORCE

Belle Gunness didn't rely solely on poison to dispatch her victims. She also employed blunt force—an equally brutal and effective method. The selection of weapons she used for these attacks was both practical and opportunistic. Hammers and axes, common tools on any farm, became lethal instruments in her hands. These tools were readily available and easily explained away as necessary for her daily farm work, making them ideal for her purposes. In addition to these, Belle also utilized heavy household objects like cast iron pans and fireplace pokers. These items, while seemingly mundane, could deliver fatal blows when wielded with intent. The environment of the farm provided an array of improvisational weapons, from wooden beams to large stones, all of which could be used to inflict deadly injuries.

The decision to use blunt force was often born out of necessity. If a victim proved more resistant or if time was a factor, Belle would resort to a quick, decisive strike. Her knowledge of anatomy, likely gleaned from years of farm work and tending to livestock, allowed her to target vulnerable areas of the body with precision. The switch from poison to brute force showed Belle's adaptability and her willingness to use whatever means necessary to maintain control.

The execution of these blunt-force attacks was marked by Belle's meticulous planning and ruthless efficiency. Timing was crucial. Belle often chose late-night hours or early morning, times when her victims would be isolated and vulnerable. The locations of the attacks were equally strategic. She preferred secluded areas of the farm, such as the barn or a remote part of the property, where the sounds of struggle would be less likely to attract attention. In these quiet corners, away from prying eyes, Belle could carry out her deadly deeds with minimal risk of interruption. Specific instances highlight her calculated approach. For example, Peter Gunness, her second husband, was reportedly struck with a meat grinder, a tool that was both lethal and conveniently at hand in their kitchen. The attack was swift, leaving little chance for resistance or outcry.

Peter Gunness

Concealing the injuries caused by blunt force trauma required a blend of pragmatism and deception. After delivering the fatal blows, Belle took great care in cleaning and washing the bodies to remove any immediate signs of violence. This initial cleanup was crucial in preventing any suspicions during the preliminary examination of the bodies. For more apparent injuries, Belle would dress the wounds to make them appear accidental. She might wrap a head wound in a bandage and claim the victim had fallen or cover bruises with clothing to obscure them from view. Quicklime, a substance used to hasten decomposition, played a significant role in her concealment efforts. By applying quicklime to the bodies, she ensured that the evidence of blunt force trauma would degrade rapidly, making it difficult for any post-mortem examination to determine the exact cause of death.

Her use of quicklime was not merely a practical choice but a testament to Belle's understanding of the decay process. She applied the substance generously, ensuring that any traces of struggle or violence would be erased before curious eyes could uncover them. The strategic placement of bodies under disturbed earth or areas frequented by animals ensured that even if remains were discovered, they would be unrecognizable and devoid of any telling signs of violence.

Managing potential resistance from her victims was another aspect of Belle's deadly strategy. To minimize the risk of struggle, Belle often incapacitated her victims before delivering the fatal blows. She would use drugs or alcohol to render them unconscious or significantly impaired. This initial incapacitation ensured that the victims were unable to defend themselves or call for help. When it came time to strike, Belle acted with swift and decisive force, delivering blows that were both lethal and quick. Her knowledge of human anatomy allowed her to target vulnerable areas, ensuring that her attacks were immediately incapacitating. In some cases, Belle may have had assistance in subduing her victims. Ray Lamphere, her farmhand and occasional lover, is suspected to have played a role in some of the murders, providing distractions or physical aid as needed.

Ray Lamphere

The combination of these strategies—carefully chosen weapons, strategic execution, meticulous concealment, and effective subduing techniques—allowed Belle Gunness to carry out her murders with chilling efficiency. Her ability to blend lethal intent with pragmatic action made her a formidable and elusive killer. Each element of her approach was designed to ensure success while minimizing the risk of detection. The farm, with its array of tools and secluded spaces, provided the perfect backdrop for her brutal methods. As you consider the intricate details of Belle's use of blunt force, reflect on the cold calculation and ruthless efficiency that defined her actions. The seemingly benign tools of farm life became instruments of death in her hands, turning the idyllic setting of La Porte into a hidden chamber of horrors.

DISPOSAL METHODS

Belle Gunness's farm was a place where life could be snuffed out, and evidence could be expertly hidden. The sprawling property in La Porte, Indiana, became a graveyard for many unsuspecting victims. Belle's methods for disposing of bodies were as varied as they were gruesome. She buried many of her victims on the property, choosing specific locations such as under the hog pen and in the garden. These spots were not chosen at random. Under the hog pen, the ground was frequently disturbed by the rooting pigs, making it an ideal location to hide the freshly dug graves. In the garden, the constant tilling of the soil provided a natural cover for her sinister activities.

The depth of the graves was another critical factor. Belle ensured that the graves were deep enough to prevent accidental discovery but shallow enough to facilitate quick digging. She often used quicklime, a substance that accelerates the decomposition of organic matter. By sprinkling quicklime over the bodies, she hastened their decay, making it less likely for anyone to identify them later. This method not only concealed the physical evidence but also masked the smell of decomposition, preventing the odor from alerting neighbors or passersby.

Burning the remains of her victims was another method Belle employed. On several occasions, she created burn piles or pyres on the property. These were typically situated in remote areas of the farm, away from the main house and out of sight of the road. She used accelerants, such as kerosene or gasoline, to ensure that the bodies burned completely. The intense heat from these fires reduced the bodies to ashes, which Belle then disposed of in various ways. She scattered some of the ashes across the fields while others were hidden in less conspicuous locations, ensuring that no trace of her victims remained.

Dismemberment was a more brutal and labor-intensive method Belle used to conceal her crimes. When she chose this approach, she employed various tools, including saws and knives, to cut the bodies into smaller, more manageable pieces. These dismembered parts were then hidden in different locations around the farm. Some were thrown into wells, where the deep water and narrow openings made retrieval nearly impossible. Others were concealed in outhouses or buried in different parts of the property. Belle's goal was to ensure that even if parts of a body were discovered, they would be unidentifiable and disconnected, reducing the chances of linking them back to her.

The dismemberment process was as methodical as her murders. Belle took care to separate the parts in a way that would make it nearly impossible to piece them back together if found. Wells and outhouses were particularly favored for disposal, as they provided both a physical barrier and an element of isolation, ensuring that even if remains were discovered, they would be impossible to recover or identify. This fragmented approach mirrored Belle's ability to compartmentalize her life—both literally and figuratively.

Avoiding detection during the disposal of bodies required careful planning and execution. Belle often chose to dispose of the bodies at night or during bad weather when the likelihood of being seen was minimal. The cover of darkness and the noise of rain or wind helped to mask the sounds of her activities. She also employed various tactics to distract neighbors and potential witnesses. On nights when she needed to dispose of a body, Belle might host a social gathering, ensuring that neighbors were preoccupied and less likely to notice any unusual activity. The layout of the farm itself was advantageous. With its sprawling fields and dense wooded areas, there were plenty of secluded spots where Belle could carry out her grim tasks without fear of interruption.

Belle's ability to use the farm's layout to her advantage was another testament to her cunning. She knew the property intimately, understanding which areas were least likely to attract attention. The natural barriers provided by the landscape, such as thick underbrush and uneven terrain, offered additional concealment. Belle's knowledge extended to the habits of the local wildlife as well. She was aware that the presence of scavengers could help in further disposing of remains, ensuring that even the smallest trace of her victims would be consumed and carried away.

In piecing together the methods Belle Gunness used to dispose of her victims, one is struck by the cold calculation and ruthless efficiency that defined her actions. Each method was chosen for its effectiveness, ensuring that the evidence of her crimes was concealed, degraded, or destroyed. The farm, with its seemingly idyllic setting, was transformed into a hidden graveyard, a place where the line between life and death was blurred by the dark ingenuity of its owner.

THE ROLE OF ACCOMPLICES

Belle Gunness, as cunning as she was ruthless, did not always operate alone. One of the most known accomplices was Ray Lamphere, her farmhand and occasional lover. Ray's relationship with Belle was complex. Initially, he was drawn to her charm and promises of love but soon found himself entangled in her web of deceit and murder. Belle manipulated Ray by offering him a semblance of affection and the promise of financial rewards. His role on the farm extended beyond typical duties. Ray assisted in the physical act of murder, helping Belle to subdue and sometimes even kill her victims. His familiarity with the farm and its operations made him an invaluable asset, albeit an unwitting one at times.

There were also other farmhands and temporary workers who might have unknowingly played a part in Belle's sinister activities. These individuals, hired for short-term tasks, could have been used to dig graves or move heavy objects without realizing the true purpose of their labor. Belle's ability to compartmentalize her operations ensured that these workers never saw the full picture. The community of La Porte itself, with its tight-knit nature, may have unwittingly assisted Belle. Neighbors who lent a hand during busy farming periods or who visited for social gatherings were kept in the dark about the true nature of Belle's activities. Their willingness to help a seemingly respectable widow only served to further Belle's deadly agenda.

Belle was skilled at delegating specific tasks to her accomplices, ensuring their involvement without exposing the full extent of her plans. Ray Lamphere, for example, was often tasked with the gruesome job of body disposal and cleanup. He would help bury the bodies or assist in burning remains, all under Belle's strict supervision. Ray's knowledge of the farm's layout made him particularly useful in these tasks. Additionally, Belle relied on Ray to provide alibis or mislead authorities. When suspicion arose, Ray would support Belle's fabricated stories, reinforcing her innocence. His loyalty, driven by a mix of fear and misguided affection, made him a reliable, if tragic, accomplice.

Yet, even with Ray's help, Belle never fully trusted him. She kept key details of her plans hidden, manipulating him with promises and half-truths to ensure his loyalty while maintaining her own power. Ray, blinded by his feelings for Belle, never realized the full extent of his role in her deadly enterprise. Belle's ability to keep her accomplices in the dark, feeding them just enough information to keep them compliant, demonstrated the depth of her control and her mastery of psychological manipulation.

Belle's manipulation of her accomplices was multifaceted. She promised Ray money and a future together, creating an illusion of love and partnership. This emotional manipulation kept him tied to her despite the growing danger. Belle also used threats and coercion to ensure compliance. Ray knew that crossing Belle could result in his own demise. Psychological manipulation was another tool in Belle's arsenal. She exerted control over Ray's thoughts and actions, making him believe that he was an integral part of her plans and that their success depended on his cooperation. This psychological grip kept Ray ensnared, even as he became increasingly aware of the deadly game he was part of.

The legal and social repercussions for Belle's known accomplices were severe. Ray Lamphere faced the brunt of the consequences. After the fire at Belle's farmhouse, Ray was arrested and charged with arson and murder. During his trial, he maintained his innocence regarding the murders, claiming he only assisted in the disposal of bodies and was unaware of Belle's full intentions. Despite his claims, Ray was convicted of arson and sentenced to prison, where he later died of tuberculosis. The community's reaction to Ray's involvement was one of shock and betrayal. Neighbors who had trusted him were horrified to learn of his complicity. Belle, however, managed to distance herself from Ray's actions. She portrayed him as a disgruntled former employee, bitter over being dismissed from the farm. This tactic allowed Belle to shift the blame and avoid direct implication in the crimes.

Belle's ability to manipulate and distance herself from her accomplices ensured that she remained a step ahead of the law. Her cunning use of emotional and psychological tactics kept her accomplices loyal, even as they faced legal repercussions. Ray Lamphere's tragic end serves as a stark reminder of the lengths Belle went to protect herself and her deadly secrets. As you continue to uncover the layers of Belle Gunness's crimes, consider the intricate web of manipulation and deceit she wove around those who became unwilling participants in her dark endeavors.

In exploring the methods Belle Gunness used to commit her crimes, it's clear that her cunning and ruthlessness knew no bounds. The role of accomplices in her murderous activities further highlights her ability to manipulate and control those around her. As you move forward, consider how these methods and manipulations allowed Belle to evade capture for so long and the impact her actions had on the community of La Porte. The next chapter will delve into the forensic challenges of the early 20th century and how they played a role in allowing Belle Gunness to continue her deadly spree.

CHAPTER 5
GENDER DYNAMICS AND SOCIETAL NORMS

Belle Gunness's story is not just a tale of murder and deception. It's also a testament to the complex gender dynamics and societal norms of early 20th-century America. To fully understand Belle's actions, you must first grasp the world she lived in —a world where women's roles were largely confined to the home, and societal expectations were both rigid and restrictive.

WOMEN'S ROLES IN EARLY 1900S AMERICA

At the dawn of the 20th century, the roles of women were clearly defined and tightly controlled by societal expectations. Women were primarily seen as homemakers, responsible for maintaining the household and raising children. The domestic responsibilities were not just demanding, they were all-encompassing, leaving little room for personal ambition or independence. A woman's value was often measured by her ability to keep a tidy home and raise well-mannered children. This societal pressure to conform to domestic roles was immense, and stepping outside these boundaries was not just frowned upon, it was often met with harsh criticism and ostracization.

Career opportunities for women were severely limited. The few who sought employment were generally restricted to roles in teaching, nursing, or domestic work. Teaching was considered an extension of a woman's nurturing role, and nearly all female teachers worked in primary schools, educating young children. Nursing was another acceptable profession, as it aligned with the caregiving aspect of womanhood. Domestic service, however, was the largest employer of women. Many young, unmarried women worked as maids, cooks, or nannies, often living in the homes of their employers. These roles, while providing some financial independence, still kept women in subservient positions. The social norms demanded modesty and submissiveness from women, reinforcing the notion that their primary duty was to support their husbands and families. The opportunities for women to break free from these roles were few and far between, and the consequences of doing so were often severe.

However, the cracks in these rigid expectations were beginning to show. As urbanization and industrialization brought new opportunities and challenges, some women began to push the boundaries of these societal norms. For women like Belle, who had seen the power and financial control men wielded, the prospect of independence—though rare—offered a glimpse of a life where she wasn't constrained by her gender. The frustration with these limitations might have contributed to her ambitions, driving her to claim her own form of control, albeit through dark means.

Legal and economic constraints further limited women's opportunities. Property rights and inheritance laws were heavily skewed in favor of men. In many cases, women could not own property independently, and any assets they brought into a marriage became the property of their husbands. Wage disparities were stark, with women earning significantly less than men for the same work. Employment restrictions were rampant, with many professions entirely closed off to women. Perhaps most glaring was the lack of voting rights. Despite organized campaigns for women's suffrage beginning as early as 1866, women did not gain the right to vote until 1920. This absence of political representation meant that women had little say in the laws and policies that governed their lives.

Cultural influences played a significant role in reinforcing these gender roles. Domestic manuals and guides were widely circulated, offering detailed instructions on how to be the perfect wife and mother. Literature and media of the time often depicted women in traditional roles, emphasizing their duties within the home. Popular novels, newspapers, and magazines were filled with stories and articles that glorified domestic life and reinforced the idea that a woman's place was in the home. Religious teachings also played a crucial role in shaping gender expectations. Many religious doctrines emphasized the importance of female modesty, obedience, and piety. These teachings permeated every aspect of society, from the pulpit to the classroom, reinforcing the belief that women should be submissive and supportive rather than ambitious and independent.

Against this backdrop, the early stirrings of the feminist movement began to take shape. Key figures and organizations emerged, advocating for women's rights and challenging societal norms. The suffrage movement gained momentum, with women organizing rallies, marches, and petitions to demand the right to vote. Leaders like Susan B. Anthony and Elizabeth Cady Stanton became prominent voices in the fight for gender equality. Their efforts began to shift societal perceptions slowly but surely. Women started to question their roles and seek greater independence and representation. The impact of these movements was not just significant; it was revolutionary, paving the way for a future where women's rights and opportunities would be more equal.

For someone like Belle Gunness, these feminist ideas were both a beacon of possibility and a source of inner conflict. While it's unclear how much Belle was directly influenced by the feminist movement, the changing societal landscape would have undoubtedly impacted her worldview. The possibilities presented by the suffrage movement and the push for women's rights might have fueled Belle's ambitions, driving her to seek financial independence and control over her own destiny. However, the restrictive societal norms and legal constraints of the time also created immense pressure, contributing to the complex psychological landscape that underpinned her actions.

As you reflect on Belle Gunness's life and crimes, consider how the societal expectations and gender dynamics of early 20th-century America shaped her actions. The rigid roles and limited opportunities for women created an environment where someone like Belle could manipulate societal norms to her advantage, using both her understanding of gender expectations and her defiance of them to carry out her deadly schemes.

BELLE AS A FEMME FATALE

The concept of the femme fatale has long fascinated both literature and history. A femme fatale is a woman who uses her allure and cunning to manipulate and ultimately destroy those who fall under her spell. She embodies danger, seduction, and manipulation, often leading men to their doom with a mix of charm and deceit. Historically and in literature, femme fatales are portrayed as cunning, seductive, and ultimately dangerous. Characters like Cleopatra, who used her beauty and wit to manipulate powerful men, and literary figures like Lady Macbeth, who pushed her husband into committing regicide, are classic examples. Belle Gunness fits this archetype seamlessly, her actions and persona aligning perfectly with this darkly captivating figure.

Belle's seductive tactics were key to her deadly success. She used her charm and attractiveness to lure her victims, presenting herself as a loving and devoted widow. Her flirtatious behavior was disarming, making her suitors believe they had found a genuine partner. Belle promised marriage and a blissful future, painting a picture of domestic tranquility. She created an inviting facade, complete with a cozy home and the promise of shared prosperity. This illusion of domestic bliss was a powerful tool, one that drew her victims into her orbit and made them vulnerable to her manipulative schemes. Her emotional manipulation was masterful. Belle knew how to exploit the desires and insecurities of her suitors, using their longing for companionship and stability to her advantage.

Her manipulation of gender roles was central to her strategy. Belle weaponized society's assumptions about women, using her perceived helplessness as a widow to make her victims lower their guard. In an era when women were largely seen as incapable of violence or deception, Belle exploited these stereotypes, becoming an unexpected predator in a world where men had little reason to fear women. Her ability to blend traditional feminine charm with cold calculation gave her a significant advantage, enabling her to commit her crimes with little initial suspicion.

Belle's actions were a stark contradiction to the gender norms of her time. In an era when women were expected to be submissive and modest, Belle was assertive and dominant. She took control of her life and finances, defying societal expectations. Her financial independence was both a means to an end and a statement of defiance. Belle's use of violence and manipulation set her apart from the typical female criminal. She employed tactics more commonly associated with male criminals, displaying a ruthlessness that shocked those around her. Belle's ability to combine traditional feminine charm with ruthless ambition made her a formidable and dangerous figure.

Society was both fascinated and horrified by Belle Gunness's crimes. Her actions challenged the conventional perceptions of female capability and danger. The public was shocked that a woman could commit such heinous acts, and this shock fueled a fascination with her story. Belle's crimes forced society to confront the uncomfortable reality that women, too, could be capable of extreme violence and manipulation. This shift in perception had a lasting impact on how female criminals were viewed. Belle's story influenced future portrayals of female criminals, both in media and in public consciousness. She became a symbol of the femme fatale, a figure who used her gender and societal expectations to her advantage, subverting norms and defying expectations.

The contrast between Belle's outward image and the brutal reality of her actions was a source of endless fascination for the media. In a society where women were supposed to embody nurturing and care, Belle's ruthlessness defied every expectation. This gendered framing of her crimes heightened the shock value, feeding into the media frenzy.

Her gender wasn't just a side note—it became central to the narrative, reinforcing the sensationalism surrounding her case.

Belle Gunness's story is a compelling example of how one woman defied societal norms to become one of history's most notorious criminals. Her ability to manipulate and control those around her, combined with her ruthless ambition, made her a true femme fatale. As you delve deeper into Belle's life, consider how she used her charm and cunning to navigate a world that sought to confine her. Reflect on the ways in which her actions challenged societal perceptions of female capability and danger, leaving a lasting impact on how female criminals are viewed. Belle Gunness was not just a murderer; she was a complex and captivating figure who defied the norms of her time to become a symbol of the dark allure of the femme fatale.

MEDIA PORTRAYAL OF FEMALE CRIMINALS

When news of Belle Gunness's crimes reached the public, newspapers and other media outlets erupted with sensational headlines and articles. The farmhouse fire, the discovery of numerous bodies, and the mystery surrounding Belle's fate were all fodder for a press eager to captivate and shock its audience. Articles often led with lurid details, emphasizing the gruesome nature of the crimes and the sheer number of victims. The media painted Belle as a monstrous figure, but they didn't stop there. Her gender and appearance were frequently highlighted, adding an extra layer of intrigue to the story. Descriptions of Belle's physicality, often exaggerated, played into the public's fascination with her persona.

Her appearance and charm were used to craft a narrative that fit the archetype of the 'deadly woman,' a seductive figure who could lead men astray. Headlines exaggerated her femininity, casting her as both a seductress and a murderer, an irresistible force whose crimes were all the more shocking because of her gender. This fixation on her appearance and femininity detracted from the complexity of her motives and methods, but it made for gripping headlines that captivated a curious and scandal-hungry public.

The focus on Belle's gender was particularly striking. The media's portrayal of her differed significantly from that of male criminals. While male murderers were often depicted as evil or insane, Belle was described with an emphasis on her femininity and seductive qualities. Headlines screamed of the "female Bluebeard," and articles dwelled on her ability to charm and deceive her victims. There was an underlying moralistic tone in many of these stories, serving as cautionary tales about the dangers of female seduction and the perils of straying from traditional gender roles. Belle was compared to other notorious female criminals of the time, such as Jane Toppan and Lizzie Borden, reinforcing the idea that women who defied societal norms were inherently dangerous.

The impact of this media coverage on public perception was profound. The sensationalized portrayal of Belle Gunness not only reinforced existing gender stereotypes but also created new ones. The public was both horrified and fascinated by the idea of a woman capable of such extreme violence. This duality of fear and fascination shaped the narrative around Belle's crimes. The media's focus on her gender and seductive qualities suggested that her criminality was an extension of her femininity, reinforcing the notion that women who stepped outside traditional roles were to be feared. This coverage contributed to a broader societal fear of female violence, casting a long shadow over how female criminals were perceived.

The lasting cultural impact of Belle Gunness's media portrayal is undeniable. Her story influenced crime literature and films for decades to come. The archetype of the femme fatale, a woman who uses her beauty and cunning to ensnare and destroy men, found a new, darker dimension in Belle's narrative. This archetype continues to captivate audiences, appearing in countless works of fiction and non-fiction. The fascination with the femme fatale extends beyond literature and film, affecting the criminal justice system's approach to female offenders. Judges, juries, and even law enforcement officers are influenced by the cultural narratives surrounding female criminals, often viewing them through a lens shaped by stories like Belle's.

The media's portrayal of Belle Gunness and other female criminals has had a lasting influence on our understanding of female criminality. By emphasizing their femininity and seductive qualities, the media created a narrative that both intrigued and terrified the public. This narrative has persisted, shaping the way we view female criminals and influencing the criminal justice system's approach to their cases. As you delve deeper into the story of Belle Gunness, consider how the media's coverage not only shaped public perception but also contributed to the enduring fascination with the dark allure of the femme fatale.

PUBLIC REACTION AND SCANDAL

The initial public reaction to the discovery of Belle Gunness's crimes was one of shock and disbelief. In the quiet community of La Porte, Indiana, neighbors and local authorities were stunned by the ghastly revelations. The image of Belle as a hardworking widow was shattered, replaced by the horrifying realization that she was a cold-blooded murderer. As authorities unearthed body after body from her farm, the local community grappled with a mix of horror and betrayal. The scale of her crimes was unprecedented, leaving residents to question how such evil could have flourished right under their noses.

News of Belle's gruesome deeds quickly spread beyond La Porte, capturing the attention of national and even international media. Newspapers from coast to coast featured front-page stories detailing the macabre discoveries and the ongoing investigation. The lurid details of the murders, combined with the mystery surrounding Belle's fate, fed a public fascination that was insatiable. People were drawn to the story not just for its horror but for the enigma of Belle Gunness herself—how could a woman commit such atrocities? The media coverage fueled a growing public obsession with the case, making Belle a household name and a symbol of female criminality.

Belle Gunness's crimes led to a moral panic that rippled through society, scandalizing communities far and wide. Public debates erupted over morality and the behavior of women, with Belle's actions serving as a focal point for broader societal anxieties. Her ability to deceive and manipulate challenged conventional notions of female innocence and virtue, prompting discussions about the true nature of women. These debates often took on an accusatory tone, with some blaming the loosening of traditional gender roles for Belle's descent into criminality. Local and national politics were not immune to the scandal. Lawmakers and public figures weighed in, using Belle's case to argue for stricter controls on women's behavior and greater oversight of female independence.

The community of La Porte, eager to distance itself from the scandal, took swift action to restore its reputation. Efforts were made to support the families of Belle's victims, providing financial aid and emotional support to those devastated by the loss of their loved ones. Public memorials and community gatherings were held to honor the victims and reassure residents that justice would be served. These efforts were aimed at healing the wounds left by Belle's actions and rebuilding the community's sense of trust and security. However, the long-term impact on La Porte's reputation was significant. The town became synonymous with the horrors of Belle Gunness's crimes, a dark chapter that would forever be a part of its history.

The reactions of the victims' families were a mix of grief and outrage. For many, the discovery of their loved ones' fates was a devastating blow, compounded by the knowledge that Belle had manipulated and betrayed them. The grief was palpable, with families struggling to come to terms with the loss and the manner in which it had occurred. Outrage was also a common response, directed not just at Belle but at the authorities who had failed to protect their loved ones. Community efforts to support these families were crucial, providing a sense of solidarity and shared mourning. The broader community also felt the impact, with many residents questioning their own complicity in allowing Belle's crimes to go unnoticed for so long.

The enduring legacy of Belle Gunness's crimes extends far beyond La Porte. Her actions challenged and ultimately changed societal norms and perceptions of female criminals. The realization that a woman could commit such heinous acts forced a reexamination of gender dynamics and societal expectations. Belle's case influenced future criminal investigations, prompting law enforcement to consider the possibility of female perpetrators in ways they had not before. Her story became a part of true crime history, a dark tale that continues to captivate and horrify. Belle Gunness remains a cultural touchstone, a reminder of the potential for darkness that exists within us all.

As you reflect on the public reaction and scandal surrounding Belle Gunness's crimes, consider the broader implications of her actions on society. The shock and disbelief, the moral panic, and the lasting impact on families and communities all serve to highlight the profound effect one individual can have on societal norms and perceptions. Belle's story is a testament to the complexity of human nature and the ways in which societal pressures can shape and sometimes distort individual behavior. Her legacy is a chilling reminder of the potential for darkness that exists within us all, a theme that will continue to unfold as we explore the forensic challenges faced by early 20th-century investigators in the next chapter.

CHAPTER 6
FORENSIC CHALLENGES

The morning after the fire at Belle Gunness's farm, investigators were greeted by a scene of utter devastation. As the ashes cooled and the first rays of sunlight pierced through the lingering smoke, a grim reality began to unfold. The farmhouse, once a symbol of rural prosperity, now lay in ruins, and with it, the charred remains of Belle's victims. The investigators knew they were facing a monumental challenge, one that would test the very limits of early 20th-century forensic science.

EARLY 20TH CENTURY FORENSICS

In the early 1900s, forensic science was still in its infancy. The field lacked the advanced tools and techniques we take for granted today. Investigators relied heavily on rudimentary methods and a limited understanding of forensic pathology. The concept of forensic pathology, which involves the study of disease and injury to determine the cause of death, was not yet fully developed. Medical examiners of the time had basic training and often lacked standardized protocols. Their ability to accurately determine the cause and manner of death was constrained by these limitations.

In some cases, local doctors, rather than formally trained forensic pathologists, were called upon to perform autopsies. Their findings, while well-meaning, were often influenced by incomplete knowledge or external pressures from the community. This led to missed signs of poisoning, internal trauma, or foul play that more advanced examinations might have revealed. The haste to declare natural causes of death over murder served to obscure Belle's role in the deaths of her suitors for a longer period.

Additionally, coroners were often political appointments rather than trained forensic professionals, which meant that crucial decisions about cause of death were sometimes left in the hands of individuals with little to no medical expertise. This lack of standardization in forensic practices made investigations prone to error and inconsistent conclusions, a vulnerability that perpetrators like Belle Gunness could exploit to continue their criminal activities unchecked.

Crime scene investigation was a far cry from the meticulous, methodical process we know today. Techniques were basic, often involving little more than sketching the scene and collecting obvious pieces of evidence. The preservation of the crime scene was a significant challenge. The lack of proper protocols meant that scenes were easily contaminated by curious onlookers or even the investigators themselves. This contamination could destroy crucial evidence, making it difficult to reconstruct events or identify suspects.

Investigators of the time relied heavily on eyewitness testimonies and confessions. These were considered the most reliable forms of evidence despite their inherent flaws. Eyewitness accounts could be influenced by a myriad of factors, including memory distortion and personal bias, while confessions were sometimes coerced, leading to false admissions of guilt. This reliance on human testimony rather than scientific analysis often resulted in flawed investigations and wrongful convictions.

Fingerprinting was one of the few forensic methods available during this era. The Henry system of fingerprint identification, developed in the late 19th century, was adopted by Scotland Yard and other law enforcement agencies around the world. This system allowed for the categorization and comparison of fingerprints, providing a reliable means of identifying individuals. However, the use of fingerprints in criminal investigations was still in its early stages. Many police departments lacked the resources or expertise to implement this technique fully.

Basic toxicology tests were another tool in the forensic arsenal. These tests could detect the presence of common poisons such as arsenic and strychnine, substances frequently used by Belle Gunness. However, toxicology in the early 1900s was limited by the sensitivity and specificity of the tests. Detecting trace amounts of poison was challenging, and false negatives were not uncommon. The crude methods for detecting bloodstains, such as the benzidine test, could indicate the presence of blood but were far from foolproof. The tests were prone to contamination and could produce false positives, complicating the interpretation of results.

Investigators faced numerous challenges due to the lack of advanced forensic tools. One of the most significant hurdles was the difficulty in preserving crime scenes. The chaotic nature of the Gunness farm after the fire made it nearly impossible to maintain the integrity of the scene. Curious neighbors and reporters trampled over potential evidence, and the fire itself had already destroyed or obscured many clues. The limited ability to analyze trace evidence further hampered the investigation. Without sophisticated techniques to examine fibers, hair, or microscopic residues, investigators were left with only the most obvious pieces of evidence.

In a crime scene as compromised as Belle's farm, every potential clue was critical. Investigators, lacking knowledge of how to protect the scene or properly analyze the debris, missed vital forensic links. Fibers, footprints, or even soil disturbances could have provided insights into movements around the farm, yet early investigators often lacked the capacity to properly interpret such details. This left many questions unanswered, prolonging the mystery surrounding the victims' identities and the full extent of Belle's crimes.

The inability to accurately determine the time of death was another critical limitation. Modern forensic science uses a combination of factors, such as body temperature (algor mortis), the pooling of blood (livor mortis), and the stiffening of muscles (rigor mortis), to estimate the time since death. In the early 1900s, these concepts were poorly understood and inconsistently applied. This lack of precision made it difficult to establish timelines and connect Belle to the exact moments of her victims' deaths.

The forensic challenges specific to the Belle Gunness case were particularly daunting. The fire had left many bodies decomposed or burned beyond recognition, complicating identification efforts. The multiple victims were in various states of decay, making it difficult to piece together a coherent narrative of their deaths. The contamination of the crime scene by curious onlookers only added to the confusion.

Investigators struggled to distinguish between genuine evidence and artifacts introduced after the fire. This contamination muddied the waters, leading to potential misinterpretations and missed opportunities for crucial discoveries.

The public's fascination with Belle's case also hindered the investigation. Crowds gathered at the site, disrupting any semblance of order as people trampled over key areas of interest. Journalists, eager to capture the sensational story, unintentionally compromised evidence by moving objects or even taking items as morbid souvenirs. This chaos further blurred the lines between solid investigative leads and irreparable contamination, creating an environment where conclusive forensic results were almost impossible to attain.

Modern forensic techniques could have transformed the investigation of Belle Gunness's crimes. DNA analysis, which allows for the precise identification of individuals and the linking of suspects to crime scenes, would have been invaluable. The ability to extract and analyze DNA from even the smallest biological samples would have provided concrete evidence connecting Belle to her victims. Advanced toxicology tests could have detected minute traces of poison, confirming suspicions about the methods she used. The digital reconstruction of crime scenes, using 3D imaging and computer models, would have helped investigators visualize the events and identify key pieces of evidence. These modern advancements highlight the stark contrast between early 20th-century forensic science and today's capabilities.

The forensic challenges faced by investigators in the Belle Gunness case underscore the limitations of early 20th-century forensic science. The lack of advanced tools and techniques, combined with the chaotic nature of the crime scene, made it incredibly difficult to conduct a thorough and accurate investigation. Reflecting on these challenges allows us to appreciate the strides forensic science has made since then and the critical role it plays in modern criminal investigations.

THE ROLE OF AUTOPSIES

In the early 20th century, autopsy procedures were rudimentary and lacked the standardization seen in modern forensic science. Medical examiners often operated without a consistent set of protocols, leading to wide variations in the quality and thoroughness of postmortem examinations. The training for these examiners was limited, with many lacking specialized knowledge in forensic pathology. This lack of expertise often resulted in superficial examinations that missed critical details. Furthermore, preservation techniques for bodies were inadequate, making it difficult to maintain the integrity of the remains for extended periods. Bodies were often poorly stored, leading to rapid decomposition and the loss of valuable forensic evidence.

The autopsies conducted on Belle Gunness's victims were plagued by these limitations. The condition of the bodies, many of which were decomposed or burned, posed significant challenges. Determining the cause of death in such cases was a Herculean task. Decomposition obscured vital forensic clues, and the fire had further compromised the remains. The medical examiners struggled to provide accurate or conclusive findings. Inaccuracies in the autopsy reports were common, with many deaths attributed to vague causes like "unknown circumstances" or "possible poisoning." Local authorities, influenced by Belle's carefully cultivated reputation and the chaos of the crime scene, may have inadvertently or intentionally downplayed suspicious findings, further complicating the investigation.

The limitations of these autopsy findings had a profound impact on the investigation. Without clear determinations of cause of death, linking Belle directly to the murders became exceedingly difficult. The lack of definitive forensic evidence fueled skepticism among both the public and law enforcement. Many questioned whether Belle's involvement could be proven beyond a reasonable doubt. This uncertainty hindered the ability to build a strong case against her. The inconclusive autopsy reports allowed for alternative explanations and theories to flourish, muddying the waters and diverting attention from Belle's culpability. Investigators were left with a fragmented and incomplete picture, struggling to piece together the true extent of her crimes.

In stark contrast, modern autopsy techniques are highly advanced and standardized. Today, forensic pathologists undergo extensive training and follow rigorous protocols to ensure thorough and accurate examinations. Advanced imaging technologies, such as CT scans and MRIs, allow for detailed internal examinations without invasive procedures. These tools can reveal hidden injuries and provide a comprehensive view of the body's condition. Improved toxicology and histology tests enable the detection of a wide range of substances and microscopic changes in tissues. These advancements allow for precise determinations of cause of death, even in cases involving decomposition or extensive trauma. The standardization of procedures ensures consistency and reliability in forensic investigations, reducing the likelihood of errors and omissions.

The use of advanced imaging technologies in modern autopsies provides a level of detail that was unimaginable in Belle Gunness's time. CT scans and MRIs can detect fractures, internal bleeding, and other injuries that might be missed in a traditional autopsy. These imaging techniques also allow for the preservation of digital records, which can be reviewed and reanalyzed as new information emerges. Improved toxicology tests have revolutionized the ability to detect poisons and other substances. Modern tests can identify minute traces of toxins, providing crucial evidence in cases of suspected poisoning. Histology, the study of tissues at the microscopic level, offers additional insights into disease processes and injuries, further enhancing the accuracy of forensic examinations.

Standardized procedures and training for forensic pathologists ensure that autopsies are conducted with a high degree of professionalism and consistency. These standards reduce variability and improve the reliability of findings. In Belle's era, the lack of such standards meant that the quality of autopsies varied widely, depending on the examiner's expertise and resources. Today, the uniformity in procedures and the emphasis on continuous education enable forensic pathologists to stay abreast of the latest developments and techniques. This commitment to excellence has significantly improved the accuracy and credibility of forensic investigations.

The evolution of autopsy techniques underscores the vital role of forensic pathology in criminal investigations. The limitations faced by early 20th-century investigators highlight the challenges of working with inadequate tools and training. Modern advancements have transformed the field, providing investigators with the means to uncover the truth with greater precision and reliability. As you consider the forensic challenges in the Belle Gunness case, reflect on how far the field has come and the critical importance of continued innovation and education in forensic science.

IDENTIFYING THE VICTIMS

The task of identifying Belle Gunness's victims was fraught with challenges. Investigators faced a grim reality: many of the bodies were severely decomposed or mutilated, complicating the identification process. In the early 20th century, the lack of dental records and DNA analysis made forensic identification a daunting endeavor. Dental records, which are now a cornerstone of forensic identification, were not systematically kept or easily accessible during Belle's time. DNA analysis, which can provide definitive proof of identity, was not yet discovered. This absence of advanced forensic tools left investigators with limited options. They had to rely on more rudimentary methods, which often led to inconclusive or inaccurate identifications.

The state of the bodies further complicated identification efforts. Many were partially decomposed, burned, or dismembered, making it difficult to ascertain distinguishing features. Decomposition obscured physical characteristics while burning and dismemberment destroyed key identifiers such as facial features and fingerprints. The scarcity of personal identification documents added another layer of difficulty. Victims often arrived at Belle's farm with minimal personal belongings, leaving little for investigators to work with. This lack of documentation meant that investigators had to rely on alternative methods to establish identity.

During Belle's era, investigators used several methods to identify victims, though each had its limitations. Visual identification by family members was a common practice. Relatives were brought in to examine the remains and identify their loved ones based on clothing, personal items, or physical traits. However, this method was fraught with emotional trauma and the inherent inaccuracies of human memory. Personal belongings and clothing found with the bodies provided some clues. Items such as jewelry, wallets, and distinctive clothing could offer hints about the victim's identity. Investigators also employed limited fingerprinting techniques, but these were often hampered by the condition of the remains. Fingerprints, if available, were compared to existing records, though this method had its own set of challenges.

The Belle Gunness case presented specific issues that further hindered identification efforts. The discovery of burned and dismembered remains created immediate obstacles. The fire had reduced some bodies to unrecognizable charred fragments while dismemberment scattered parts across the property. This gruesome reality made it nearly impossible to match body parts to a single individual. The presence of multiple bodies in various states of decay added to the confusion. Investigators struggled to determine how many victims there were and which remains belonged to whom. Misidentification and false leads were common. In the chaos of the scene, it was easy for investigators to make mistakes, leading to incorrect identifications and further complicating the investigation.

Modern forensic techniques offer a stark contrast to the methods used in Belle's time. DNA profiling has revolutionized the field of forensic identification. By extracting DNA from bone or tissue samples, forensic scientists can generate a genetic profile unique to the individual. This profile can then be compared to DNA samples from potential relatives or existing databases, providing a definitive identification. Genetic genealogy, which uses DNA to trace family connections, has also become a powerful tool in solving cold cases. Advanced dental and skeletal analysis techniques provide additional avenues for identification. Forensic odontologists can compare dental records to the teeth of unidentified remains, while forensic anthropologists analyze skeletal features to determine age, sex, and ancestry.

The use of databases and digital records has further enhanced identification efforts. Databases containing dental records, medical records, and missing person reports allow investigators to cross-reference information quickly and accurately. Digital records can be easily shared and accessed by multiple agencies, streamlining the identification process. These advancements highlight the significant progress made in forensic science since the early 20th century. They underscore the challenges faced by investigators in the Belle Gunness case and the limitations of the methods available to them.

Identifying the victims of Belle Gunness was a complex and often heartbreaking task. The limitations of early 20th-century forensic science, coupled with the condition of the remains and the lack of personal identification documents, made the process incredibly challenging. Modern forensic techniques offer a glimpse into how these challenges could have been overcome, providing a deeper understanding of the difficulties faced by investigators and the impact of these advancements on the field of forensic science.

MODERN FORENSIC COMPARISONS

Forensic science has come a long way since the early 1900s. One of the most significant advancements is the development of DNA analysis. This revolutionary technique allows forensic scientists to identify individuals with astonishing accuracy. By examining the unique genetic code in biological samples, investigators can link suspects to crime scenes or identify unknown victims. DNA analysis has become a cornerstone of modern forensic investigations, providing concrete evidence that can withstand the scrutiny of the courtroom.

Enhanced forensic imaging and digital technologies have also transformed the field. Techniques like 3D scanning and digital reconstruction allow investigators to recreate crime scenes with incredible detail. These tools help visualize the sequence of events, identify critical pieces of evidence, and present findings in a clear and compelling manner. Digital records ensure that evidence can be preserved and reviewed, reducing the risk of loss or degradation over time. These technologies have made forensic investigations more precise and reliable, enabling investigators to uncover truths that would have remained hidden in the past.

Improved chemical and biological testing methods have expanded the range of substances that can be detected and analyzed. Advanced toxicology tests can identify even trace amounts of poisons, drugs, and other chemicals in biological samples. Techniques like mass spectrometry and chromatography provide detailed profiles of substances, helping to determine their origin and potential effects. Biological testing methods, including RNA profiling and forensic DNA phenotyping, offer insights into the characteristics of individuals and the types of biological materials present at a crime scene. These advancements have significantly enhanced the ability to detect and interpret forensic evidence.

If modern forensic techniques had been available during the Belle Gunness investigation, the outcomes might have been drastically different. DNA analysis could have provided definitive identification of her victims, linking them to their families and establishing the extent of her crimes. Samples from the remains, even those that were decomposed or burned, could have yielded valuable genetic information. This would have eliminated much of the guesswork and speculation that plagued the original investigation, providing clear and irrefutable evidence.

Digital reconstruction of the crime scenes could have offered a detailed overview of the events that transpired at Belle's farm. Investigators could have used 3D scanning to create models of the property, pinpointing where bodies were found and reconstructing the sequence of events leading to the murders. These visual aids would have been invaluable in understanding the layout of the farm and the logistics of Belle's crimes. They could also have been used in court to present a compelling case to the jury, helping to secure a conviction.

Advanced toxicology tests would have been crucial in detecting the presence of poisons in Belle's victims. These tests could have identified specific substances used to incapacitate and kill her victims, providing concrete evidence of her methods. The ability to detect even minute traces of poison would have strengthened the case against her, eliminating doubts about the cause of death and linking Belle directly to the murders. This forensic evidence would have been difficult for the defense to refute, increasing the likelihood of a successful prosecution.

Reflecting on the limitations of early forensic science, it's clear that many lessons have been learned. The importance of preserving crime scenes cannot be overstated. Modern forensic practices emphasize the need to secure and protect the scene to prevent contamination and loss of evidence. This principle, born out of the challenges faced by early investigators, is now a fundamental aspect of forensic investigations.

The value of multidisciplinary forensic teams has also been recognized. Combining the expertise of forensic pathologists, toxicologists, anthropologists, and other specialists ensures a comprehensive approach to criminal investigations. This collaborative effort enhances the accuracy and reliability of findings, providing a more complete understanding of the evidence. The ongoing advancements and innovations in forensic science continue to push the boundaries of what is possible, offering new tools and techniques to uncover the truth.

As we conclude this chapter on forensic challenges, it's essential to connect these lessons to the broader narrative. The limitations faced by early investigators highlight the importance of continuous improvement in forensic science. The advancements we've seen over the past century underscore the critical role of innovation in solving crimes and bringing justice to victims. In the next chapter, we'll delve into the investigation itself, examining how these forensic challenges influenced the course of events and the ultimate fate of Belle Gunness.

CHAPTER 7

THE INVESTIGATION

THE INITIAL DISCOVERY

The crisp morning air in La Porte, Indiana, was shattered by the unmistakable smell of smoke and the sight of flames licking at the sky. It was early on April 28, 1908, when the alarm was raised. Belle Gunness's farmhouse, a symbol of her supposed respectability, was engulfed in a roaring blaze. Neighbors roused from their sleep, rushed to the scene, their faces etched with shock and confusion. The fire's intensity was overwhelming, casting an eerie glow over the surrounding fields and sending sparks into the pre-dawn sky. The community, tight-knit and ever-vigilant, sprang into action, grabbing buckets and forming a makeshift brigade to combat the inferno.

Eyewitness accounts from that morning paint a picture of chaos and urgency. The first responders, a mix of neighbors and local authorities, fought valiantly to control the fire. Their efforts were hampered by the sheer ferocity of the flames, which consumed the wooden structure with alarming speed. As the fire raged, questions began to surface. How had it started? Where was Belle? And more importantly, where were her children? The absence of Belle Gunness and her family was immediately felt, casting a pall of dread over the scene. The community's initial assumption was that this was a tragic accident, a household fire that had spiraled out of control. But as the flames were eventually subdued and the smoldering ruins revealed their secrets, suspicions of foul play began to take root.

The first impressions of law enforcement were cautious yet concerned. The La Porte authorities, familiar with the Gunness household, were struck by the suddenness and severity of the blaze. Initial assumptions leaned towards an accidental fire, perhaps caused by a stove left unattended or faulty wiring. However, the absence of Belle Gunness and her children raised immediate red flags. Officers on the scene began to suspect that this was no ordinary fire. The possibility of arson loomed large, especially given Belle's contentious relationship with Ray Lamphere, a former farmhand with a known grudge. The community, too, was quick to speculate. Whispers of foul play and deliberate malice spread like wildfire, fueled by the eerie silence surrounding Belle's whereabouts.

As the smoldering wreckage was carefully examined, the grim discovery of bodies deepened the mystery. The charred remains were found in various parts of the house, each discovery more horrifying than the last. The first bodies uncovered were those of Belle's three children, their small forms huddled together as if in a final embrace. Nearby, a headless adult body was discovered, initially presumed to be Belle herself. The condition of the bodies made identification challenging. The intense heat had rendered them almost unrecognizable, complicating efforts to confirm their identities. Initial hypotheses suggested that the headless body belonged to Belle, but doubts lingered. The body's size and build did not match Belle's known stature, leading some to question whether she had, in fact, perished in the fire or staged her own death to escape justice.

As law enforcement sifted through the charred remains, they were struck by the absence of key elements that could indicate an accidental fire. No faulty wiring or obvious mechanical failure was discovered. Instead, investigators were left to wonder whether the blaze was meant to cover a darker reality, a question that would linger as more bodies were unearthed and Belle's history came under closer scrutiny.

The media's response to the fire and the subsequent discoveries was immediate and sensational. Newspapers across the country seized upon the story, their headlines screaming of murder and mystery. Articles speculated wildly about the circumstances of the fire and the fate of Belle Gunness. The public, already intrigued by tales of Belle's matrimonial schemes, was now gripped by the unfolding drama. The discovery of multiple bodies on the property only added to the fervor. Sensational headlines like "Murder Farm Exposed" and "The Devil in La Porte" dominated the news, painting Belle as a monstrous figure whose crimes defied comprehension. The media pressure on law enforcement was immense, with reporters demanding answers and fueling public outrage.

Public reaction to the news was a mix of horror, disbelief, and morbid fascination. The idea that a seemingly respectable widow could be at the center of such a gruesome saga was both shocking and titillating. Communities far beyond La Porte followed the story closely, their imaginations captured by the macabre details. The pressure on local authorities to provide answers and deliver justice was palpable. Investigators found themselves under intense scrutiny, both from the media and the public. The discovery of bodies, coupled with the suspicions of arson, transformed the investigation into a high-stakes quest for truth.

As the investigation continued, the full extent of Belle Gunness's dark deeds began to come to light. The fire, initially thought to be a tragic accident, was revealed to be a catalyst, uncovering a web of murder and deceit that had long been hidden beneath the surface. For the residents of La Porte, the revelations were a chilling reminder that even the most seemingly ordinary lives could harbor unimaginable horrors. The question of whether Belle had truly perished in the blaze or had orchestrated an elaborate escape remained unanswered, adding another layer of mystery to an already perplexing case.

THE ROLE OF RAY LAMPHERE

Ray Lamphere, a man whose life would become inextricably linked with Belle Gunness, had been employed on her farm for several years. His duties ranged from general farm labor to more personal tasks, earning him a position of trust within Belle's household. However, this trust was a double-edged sword. Ray's relationship with Belle was complex and fraught with underlying tensions. While he was drawn to her charm and the promise of a better life, he was also ensnared in her manipulative web. Belle, ever the master of deception, knew how to exploit Ray's affections and loyalty. Their relationship was not merely that of employer and employee; it was a volatile mix of romantic entanglements and power dynamics. Conflicts arose frequently, often fueled by Belle's demands and Ray's growing frustrations. These tensions eventually reached a boiling point, culminating in a fallout that would have dire consequences for Ray.

The circumstances leading to Ray Lamphere's arrest were steeped in suspicion and mounting evidence. In the days following the devastating fire at Belle's farmhouse, investigators began to piece together a troubling narrative. Eyewitness accounts and Ray's known grievances with Belle made him an immediate suspect. The discovery of incriminating evidence further sealed his fate. Among the ruins, authorities found personal items belonging to Ray, as well as cryptic notes hinting at a deeper involvement in the fire. Ray's arrest was swift, and he was taken into custody for interrogation. During this intense questioning, Ray maintained a precarious balance between denial and partial admissions. He confessed to being present at the farm on the night of the fire but vehemently denied any involvement in setting it. His responses were a mix of defensiveness and desperation, painting a picture of a man ensnared in circumstances beyond his control.

As the investigation progressed, the accusations against Ray Lamphere became more concrete. He was charged with arson, and the case against him was built on a foundation of key testimonies and physical evidence. Witnesses testified to seeing Ray near the property on the night of the fire, and experts presented findings that linked him to the scene. The trial, a spectacle in its own right, captivated the public and the media. Key moments included gripping testimonies from neighbors and forensic experts who detailed the evidence against Ray. Despite his defense team's efforts to portray him as a scapegoat, the weight of the evidence was overwhelming. Ray's defense centered on his claims of innocence and his contentious relationship with Belle. He argued that he had been framed, a victim of Belle's manipulative schemes. However, the jury was unconvinced, and Ray was ultimately found guilty of arson. He was sentenced to a lengthy prison term, a verdict that many in the community believed was justified.

Despite Ray's conviction, his trial left many unanswered questions. Some believed that while he may have started the fire, he did so under Belle's manipulation. Others posited that Ray was merely a convenient scapegoat, allowing Belle the opportunity to vanish into the shadows, escaping punishment altogether. These lingering doubts about Ray's true role cast a pall over the justice served in the case, leaving the community torn between relief and suspicion.

Ray Lamphere's involvement had a profound impact on the overall investigation. His statements during interrogation provided crucial insights into Belle's operations, shifting the focus of the investigation towards uncovering the full extent of her crimes. Ray's assertions that Belle had orchestrated the fire to cover her tracks and possibly escape added a new layer of complexity to the case. Public perception of Ray was deeply divided. Some saw him as a willing accomplice, while others believed he was merely a pawn in Belle's deadly game. This division was mirrored in the community's reaction to his conviction. Law enforcement, meanwhile, used Ray's information to guide their efforts in gathering further evidence. His involvement highlighted the need for a more thorough examination of Belle's activities, prompting a deeper and more methodical approach to the investigation.

Many locals whispered that Ray Lamphere, in a way, became the final victim of Belle's manipulations, entrapped by his love for her and ultimately taking the fall for crimes that were hers alone. Yet, some believed Ray knew much more than he let on, that he was not only complicit but an eager participant in her deadly schemes. This duality in public perception only deepened the mystery surrounding his true involvement.

Ray Lamphere's role in the Belle Gunness saga is a testament to the intricate and often dark relationships that underpinned her life. His journey from a trusted worker to a convicted arsonist illustrates the far-reaching impact of Belle's manipulations. The insights gleaned from Ray's involvement were instrumental in unraveling the full scope of Belle's crimes, yet they also underscored the complexities and challenges faced by those who fell under her spell. As you delve deeper into this investigation, consider the intricate web of deceit and control that Belle wove and how Ray's story is but one thread in the larger tapestry of her dark legacy.

THE HOUSE FIRE

The fire that consumed Belle Gunness's farmhouse erupted in the stillness of the night, its origins shrouded in mystery and speculation. Some believed it started in the kitchen, perhaps due to a stove left burning or faulty wiring, but others whispered darker theories. The sequence of events unfolded rapidly. Flames engulfed the wooden structure, spreading with a ferocity that suggested accelerants might have been used. The roaring blaze lit up the night sky, casting an eerie glow that could be seen from miles away. By the time the first responders arrived, the fire had already taken its toll, reducing the once-sturdy farmhouse to a smoldering ruin. The damage was extensive; the house was almost entirely destroyed, leaving behind only charred remnants and the skeletal framework of what had been.

Investigating the cause of the fire required a meticulous examination of the scene. Investigators first studied the fire patterns, looking for signs that would indicate how the blaze had spread. They analyzed the point of origin, trying to determine if it was indeed an accident or if it bore the hallmarks of arson. Witness statements were crucial. Neighbors recounted hearing strange noises before the fire broke out, while others reported seeing a figure moving around the property late at night. Expert analyses provided further insights, though they were hampered by the limitations of early 20th-century forensic techniques. The challenges were immense. The intense heat had obliterated much of the physical evidence, and the contamination of the scene by onlookers complicated efforts to piece together a clear narrative.

The significance of the fire in the context of Belle Gunness's crimes cannot be overstated. It obliterated critical physical evidence that could have definitively linked her to the murders. Theories about Belle's possible motives for the fire abounded. Some speculated that she had set the blaze to destroy evidence and cover her tracks, while others believed it was a desperate act to fake her death and escape justice. The fire played a pivotal role in shaping both public and investigative narratives. Initially, it prompted sympathy for Belle as a victim of a tragic accident, but as more details emerged, it became clear that the fire was part of a much more sinister plot. The discovery of bodies amid the ruins turned the narrative on its head, transforming Belle from a grieving mother to a prime suspect in a series of gruesome murders.

One particularly persistent theory was that Belle staged her own death, using the fire as a means to slip away unnoticed. The headless body discovered in the ruins, initially thought to be Belle, did not match her physical proportions. Was this a carefully calculated move to throw authorities off her trail? Or was Belle, as some still believed, truly a victim of her own dangerous web of deception? These uncertainties added fuel to an already roaring media frenzy.

The immediate aftermath of the fire left the local community in shock. Efforts to rebuild or recover from the disaster began almost immediately. Neighbors banded together, offering support to one another as they grappled with the enormity of what had happened. The community's resilience was evident in the way they rallied to support the victims' families, providing financial aid and emotional comfort. Public meetings and gatherings were held to discuss the incident, with townsfolk seeking answers and reassurance. The sense of betrayal was palpable; Belle had not only deceived her victims but had also betrayed the trust of an entire community. The fire, which had initially seemed like a tragic accident, had revealed a web of deceit and murder that shocked La Porte to its core. As the investigation continued, the true extent of Belle Gunness's crimes began to emerge, painting a chilling portrait of a woman whose capacity for evil knew no bounds.

DIGGING UP THE FARM

The decision to start digging up Belle Gunness's farm came from a series of unsettling tips and leads. Neighbors had long whispered about the men who came to visit and were never seen again. The suspicious fire that consumed her house only intensified these rumors. Authorities received a tip from Asle Helgelien, a man looking for his missing brother, Andrew, who had been corresponding with Belle before his disappearance. This tip, combined with the growing number of missing persons connected to Belle, prompted law enforcement to seek approval for a thorough excavation of the property. The planning was meticulous, involving local authorities and, eventually, state officials. The initial areas of focus were the hog pen and garden—places that seemed most likely to hide dark secrets. Given the rudimentary forensic techniques of the time, investigators faced significant challenges. The lack of sophisticated tools meant that they had to rely heavily on manual labor and the sharp eyes of the excavation team. This lack of refinement worked in Belle's favor, as it made it easier for her to conceal her crimes.

The discoveries made during the excavation were nothing short of horrifying. Over several weeks, investigators unearthed a grim tally of bodies, each more gruesome than the last. The final count stood at more than a dozen, though some estimates suggest the number could have been higher. The condition of the bodies varied; some were relatively intact, while others were dismembered and partially decomposed. The locations where the bodies were found were equally disturbing. Many victims were buried in shallow graves under the hog pen, their bodies covered with quicklime to hasten decomposition. Others were found in the garden, their remains tangled in the roots of trees and plants. Personal belongings were also discovered, providing poignant clues to the identities of the victims. Items such as watches, rings, and letters were meticulously cataloged, each piece of evidence adding to the growing case against Belle Gunness.

Andrew Helgelien

The excavation was not without its challenges. The physical difficulties of digging on the property were immense. The ground was hard and unforgiving, requiring significant effort to break through. The emotional toll on investigators and community members was also considerable. Each new discovery brought waves of grief and horror as the full extent of Belle's crimes became painfully clear. Handling the media presence was another significant challenge. Reporters flocked to La Porte, eager for the latest grisly details. Their constant presence added pressure to an already tense situation, forcing investigators to balance the need for thoroughness with the public's demand for answers. The curiosity of the townspeople also had to be managed, as many flocked to the site, drawn by morbid fascination.

Despite efforts to keep the investigation methodical, the overwhelming media presence frequently interrupted the dig. Reporters from national newspapers pressed for access, hoping for firsthand glimpses of the grim discoveries, while townspeople fueled by morbid curiosity crowded around the farm, turning the dig site into an unwelcome spectacle. This pressure made it increasingly difficult for investigators to keep their focus on uncovering the truth, as they had to navigate the chaos of prying eyes while maintaining the dignity of the deceased.

The impact of the discoveries on the investigation was profound. Each body unearthed strengthened the case against Belle Gunness, painting a clearer picture of her murderous activities. The physical evidence, combined with the personal belongings found with the victims, provided irrefutable proof of her guilt. New leads and connections were uncovered as well. Letters and documents found on the property pointed to other potential victims and provided insights into Belle's methods. The media coverage shifted dramatically. Initially focused on the fire, the narrative quickly changed to one of a cold-blooded serial killer. Public interest soared, with newspapers across the country dedicating front-page stories to the unfolding horror in La Porte. This increased scrutiny put additional pressure on law enforcement to deliver a comprehensive and thorough investigation.

The chapter reveals the sheer scale of Belle Gunness's crimes and the painstaking efforts required to uncover the truth. The discoveries at the farm not only solidified Belle's infamy but also highlighted the limitations of early forensic science. Each body found was a testament to her cunning and ruthlessness. As you move forward, the story will delve into the broader implications of Belle's actions, exploring how her case challenged societal norms and reshaped the understanding of female criminality.

CHAPTER 8
TRIALS AND LEGAL PROCEEDINGS

The trial of Ray Lamphere began under a cloud of intense public scrutiny and media frenzy. The courtroom was packed, the atmosphere electric with anticipation. For the residents of La Porte, Indiana, and the curious onlookers from far and wide, this trial was more than a legal proceeding—it was a spectacle, a drama that promised to reveal the dark truths hidden within Belle Gunness's murder farm.

RAY LAMPHERE'S TRIAL

Ray Lamphere's trial commenced on November 13, 1908, and stretched over several grueling weeks. The courtroom became a theater of accusation and defense, with key figures playing their parts in this high-stakes drama. Presiding over the case was Judge Richter, a stern figure determined to see justice served. On one side stood the prosecution, led by District Attorney Ralph Smith, a man with a reputation for tenacity and precision. On the other, defending Ray, was attorney Wirt Worden, whose task was to dismantle the prosecution's narrative and present Ray as a victim of Belle Gunness's manipulations. The charges against Ray were severe: arson, conspiracy, and complicity in the murders that had shocked the nation. The stakes couldn't have been higher.

The opening statements set the tone for the trial, painting a stark contrast between the prosecution's portrayal of Ray as an accomplice and arsonist and the defense's depiction of him as an innocent pawn. District Attorney Smith began with a compelling narrative, describing Ray as a willing participant in Belle's gruesome deeds. He painted a picture of a man who had aided and abetted Belle in her murderous schemes, driven by a mix of fear and infatuation. The prosecution's strategy was clear: to link Ray directly to the fire that had consumed Belle's farmhouse and the subsequent discovery of the bodies. The defense, however, countered with a narrative steeped in tragedy and manipulation. Attorney Worden argued that Ray was a victim, ensnared by Belle's charms and caught in a web of deceit. He presented Ray as a simple man, led astray by a calculating and ruthless woman. The public and media reacted with a mix of skepticism and empathy, the courtroom buzzing with speculation and debate.

Worden's defense strategy hinged on painting Belle as the true mastermind, a cold-hearted woman who toyed with Ray's emotions and used his infatuation to her advantage. He described Ray as a man entrapped by Belle's seductive promises and eventually discarded when he became inconvenient. As Worden spoke, the courtroom was silent, captivated by the portrait of Ray as the tragic victim of a calculating femme fatale. The defense argued that it was Belle, not Ray, who had orchestrated the fire as a means to escape justice, leaving Ray to face the consequences.

The prosecution's case was built on a foundation of witness testimonies and physical evidence. They called upon neighbors who had seen Ray near the farm on the night of the fire, their accounts painting a damning picture. These witnesses described Ray's movements with a level of detail that lent credibility to the prosecution's claims. Furthermore, the prosecution presented evidence of Ray's tumultuous relationship with Belle. They highlighted past conflicts and tensions, portraying Ray as a man with a motive to commit arson. Physical evidence also played a crucial role. Items found at the scene of the fire, including charred remains of personal belongings linked to Ray, were methodically presented to the jury. Each piece of evidence added weight to the argument that Ray was not just an innocent bystander but an active participant in the crimes.

The defense's strategy was to poke holes in the prosecution's narrative and sow doubt in the minds of the jurors. Attorney Worden worked tirelessly to discredit the witness testimonies, suggesting that the neighbors' accounts were influenced by the chaos and confusion of the fire. He questioned their reliability, pointing out inconsistencies and highlighting the lack of direct evidence linking Ray to the arson. The defense also focused on portraying Ray as a scapegoat. They argued that Belle, known for her manipulative prowess, had set Ray up to take the fall. Worden presented Ray as a man trapped by circumstances beyond his control, a victim of Belle's cunning schemes. Character witnesses were called to attest to Ray's generally good nature and lack of criminal intent. These testimonies aimed to humanize Ray and cast doubt on the prosecution's depiction of him as a willing accomplice.

The defense even suggested that Belle had a history of manipulation, pointing to the many men who had disappeared after visiting her farm. Worden asserted that Ray, like those men, had been lured into Belle's world with promises of love and prosperity, only to find himself ensnared in a deadly game. It was a bold tactic, one that sought to shift the blame entirely onto Belle, even though she was no longer present to defend herself.

The trial's atmosphere was charged with tension, each day bringing new revelations and shifting public opinion. For true crime enthusiasts, the unfolding drama offered a window into the dark world of Belle Gunness and the complexities of her relationships. Historical crime buffs found the trial a fascinating glimpse into early 20th-century legal proceedings, while psychological thriller fans were drawn to the intricate profiles of both Ray and Belle. Feminist readers saw in Belle's story a stark defiance of societal norms, and media examiners analyzed the sensational coverage's impact on the trial's proceedings. For amateur sleuths, each testimony and piece of evidence was a puzzle piece, inviting them to piece together the truth in a case shrouded in mystery and deception.

TESTIMONIES AND EVIDENCE

As the trial of Ray Lamphere unfolded, the courtroom became a theater of human drama, where the past lives of those entangled with Belle Gunness were laid bare. Key testimonies from witnesses painted vivid pictures of the events leading up to the fire and the complex relationships that Belle had woven around her.

Neighbors were among the first to take the stand, their testimonies echoing through the packed courtroom. They recounted heated arguments between Ray and Belle, confrontations that had often spilled out into the open, audible to anyone nearby. One neighbor recalled a particularly intense quarrel, describing how Belle's voice had risen in anger, only to be met with Ray's desperate pleas. These testimonies provided a glimpse into the volatile relationship between Belle and Ray, suggesting that their interactions were far from harmonious. The prosecution used these accounts to argue that Ray's frustrations had boiled over, leading him to commit arson in a fit of rage.

One particularly damning testimony came from a farmhand who described overhearing Belle threaten Ray. According to the witness, Belle had warned Ray that she could 'dispose of him as easily as the others,' a chilling statement that painted Belle as a woman unafraid to eliminate those who crossed her. The prosecution seized on this testimony, arguing that Ray had become so fearful of Belle that he saw arson as his only way out.

Former farmhands also offered their insights into Ray's behavior. They spoke of Ray's increasing agitation in the weeks leading up to the fire. One farmhand described how Ray had become more erratic, often muttering to himself about Belle's demands and the fear she instilled in him. Another recounted how Ray had confided in him about feeling trapped and manipulated by Belle. These statements painted Ray as a man under immense psychological strain, torn between his loyalty to

Belle and his growing resentment. The prosecution seized upon these testimonies to further their argument that Ray had both motive and opportunity to set the fire.

Eyewitness accounts of Ray's actions on the day of the fire were particularly damning. Several witnesses testified to seeing Ray near the farm in the hours before the blaze began. One witness described how he had seen Ray carrying what appeared to be a container of kerosene, a detail that aligned with the prosecution's theory of arson. Another witness, a local shopkeeper, testified that Ray had purchased matches and flammable materials from his store the previous day. These accounts provided a timeline that placed Ray squarely at the scene, reinforcing the prosecution's narrative of premeditated arson.

Forensic evidence presented in court further complicated Ray's defense. Fire debris analysis revealed traces of accelerants, supporting the theory that the fire had been deliberately set. The prosecution argued that these accelerants were consistent with the materials Ray had been seen carrying. Medical examination reports on the bodies found in the aftermath of the fire added another layer of complexity. The condition of the remains, particularly the absence of Belle's head, suggested foul play. However, forensic limitations of the time meant that conclusive identification was challenging, leaving room for doubt.

Belle's letters and documents played a pivotal role in the trial. Love letters between Belle and Ray were introduced as evidence, revealing a relationship marked by emotional manipulation. These letters, filled with Belle's promises and demands, illustrated how she had ensnared Ray in her web. Financial documents uncovered during the investigation indicated Belle's elaborate schemes to defraud her suitors. The prosecution used these documents to argue that Belle had orchestrated a broader conspiracy, with Ray as her unwitting accomplice. Letters to potential victims, many of whom had met tragic ends, underscored Belle's manipulative prowess and provided context for her interactions with Ray.

When Ray Lamphere took the stand, the courtroom was hushed. His testimony was a blend of desperation and defiance. Ray claimed innocence, portraying himself as a victim of Belle's machinations. He recounted his relationship with Belle, describing how she had used him to further her schemes and then discarded him when he became inconvenient. Ray spoke of his fear of Belle, recounting instances of her threats and manipulations. The prosecution's cross-examination was relentless. They sought to undermine Ray's credibility, highlighting inconsistencies in his account and questioning his motives. Despite his protestations, Ray's testimony left the jury with a complex, multifaceted portrait of a man caught in Belle's deadly orbit.

THE VERDICT

The jury deliberations in Ray Lamphere's trial were a tense and arduous process, stretching over several days. The jurors, sequestered away from the public eye, grappled with the weight of their decision. They were tasked with sifting through a mountain of evidence and conflicting testimonies to determine Ray's fate. The deliberation room buzzed with heated debates and intense discussions. Jurors argued over key points, such as the reliability of witness testimonies and the physical evidence linking Ray to the fire. The public and media pressure loomed large, a constant, invisible presence that added to the stress of their task. The jurors knew that their decision would not only impact Ray Lamphere's life but also shape the narrative surrounding one of the most sensational cases in Indiana's history.

The atmosphere in the courtroom was thick with tension and anticipation as the jury filed back in to announce their verdict. Spectators held their breath, the silence almost palpable. Ray Lamphere, seated with his defense team, wore a mask of stoic composure, though his eyes betrayed a flicker of fear. District Attorney Ralph Smith and his team stood ready, their expressions a mix of confidence and apprehension. Judge Richter, overseeing the proceedings with a stern gaze, called for order as the jury foreman rose to deliver the verdict. The room seemed to contract, every eye fixed on the foreman as he read the words that would seal Ray's fate. The verdict: guilty of arson. The courtroom erupted in a cacophony of reactions—gasps, murmurs, and the occasional cry of disbelief. Ray's defense team immediately huddled, discussing their next steps, while

Ray himself seemed to sag under the weight of the decision. The prosecution exchanged satisfied nods, their hard-fought battle yielding the outcome they had sought. Judge Richter maintained order, his gavel striking sharply to silence the room.

The sentencing phase followed swiftly, a somber formality that underscored the gravity of the verdict. Judge Richter addressed the court, his voice steady and authoritative. He spoke of the heinous nature of the crimes associated with Belle Gunness and the fire that had claimed innocent lives. The judge emphasized the need for justice, not just for the victims but for the community that had been torn apart by these events. Ray Lamphere was sentenced to a lengthy prison term, a fate that many believed he had narrowly escaped before. In addition to the prison sentence, fines were imposed, meant to serve as a further deterrent to any who might contemplate similar crimes. Ray's response to the sentencing was muted; he stood quietly, his face a canvas of resignation and defeat as the reality of his situation sank in.

The immediate aftermath of the verdict was a whirlwind of emotions and reactions. Ray's family and supporters were devastated, their hopes for acquittal shattered. Some wept openly, while others stood in stunned silence. The prosecutors and investigators, while relieved by the outcome, were acutely aware that their work was far from over. Statements made to the press were measured, emphasizing the importance of the verdict in bringing some measure of justice to the victims. Media coverage was relentless, with headlines blaring the news of Ray's conviction. Public opinion shifted rapidly, with some seeing the verdict as a just end to a tragic chapter, while others remained unconvinced of Ray's guilt, believing him to be another victim of Belle Gunness's manipulative schemes. The trial's conclusion did little to quell the ongoing fascination with the case, leaving many questions unanswered and the true extent of Belle Gunness's crimes still shrouded in mystery.

Supporters of Ray clung to the belief that he had been unfairly prosecuted, pointing to the lack of concrete evidence directly linking him to the arson. They argued that Ray was a convenient scapegoat, chosen to placate the public's desire for justice. Meanwhile, others felt a deep sense of betrayal, wondering how someone they had known for years could have been involved in such heinous crimes. Ray's conviction left a deep scar, both for his family and for the community.

For many in La Porte, the trial's conclusion did not bring the closure they had hoped for. While Ray had been convicted of arson, doubts lingered about his role in the murders. Some believed that Belle had manipulated him into taking the fall, while others remained convinced that Ray was an accomplice in her gruesome deeds. The debate continued in homes and cafes across the country, with many wondering if justice had truly been served.

PUBLIC AND MEDIA REACTION

The media's frenzy surrounding Ray Lamphere's trial was nothing short of a spectacle. Newspapers from all over the country dedicated front-page headlines to the case, with articles that ranged from sensationalist to factual. Major publications like The New York Times and the Chicago Tribune followed every twist and turn; their reporters camped outside the courthouse, eager for the latest scoop. The press painted a vivid picture of the courtroom drama, describing Ray as a tragic figure ensnared by the ruthless Belle Gunness. Sensationalist papers did not hesitate to embellish details, crafting a narrative that captivated the public's imagination. Stories of Belle's manipulative prowess and Ray's alleged complicity fed the public's hunger for scandal, shaping perceptions and fueling debates.

Public opinion was sharply divided. Supporters of Ray Lamphere believed passionately in his innocence. They saw him as another victim of Belle Gunness, a simple man manipulated by a master deceiver. These supporters held onto the hope that justice would ultimately exonerate Ray, their voices loud and insistent in the din of public discourse. Skeptics, however, viewed Ray as a convenient scapegoat, a pawn in Belle's larger game. They questioned the reliability of witness testimonies and the integrity of the investigation, arguing that Ray was being unfairly targeted to close a case that was far from resolved. In La Porte, the general sentiment was one of betrayal and confusion. The community had been torn apart by the revelations, and the trial only deepened the wounds. Discussions in local cafes and homes were fraught with tension as residents grappled with the horrifying reality that had unfolded in their midst.

The trial and its verdict had a profound impact on Belle Gunness's legacy. Far from diminishing her infamy, the proceedings reinforced the image of Belle as a manipulative mastermind. The courtroom revelations painted her in even darker hues, adding layers to the already chilling narrative. The ongoing fascination with her possible escape kept the public riveted, with many speculating whether Belle had indeed staged her own death to elude justice. This aspect of the story added an enduring mystery, one that would continue to captivate true crime enthusiasts and amateur sleuths alike. The trial also influenced future true crime narratives, setting a precedent for how female criminals were portrayed. Belle's story became a reference point, a cautionary tale that highlighted the dangers of underestimating women's capacity for violence and deceit.

As rumors swirled about Belle's possible escape, amateur sleuths and journalists alike combed through the details of the case, searching for clues. Some speculated that Belle had fled to another part of the country, living under an assumed name, while others suggested she had met a grisly fate at the hands of a jealous lover or accomplice. The uncertainty surrounding Belle's fate only added to her legend, cementing her place in the annals of true crime history.

The long-term repercussions of the trial were far-reaching, affecting legal, social, and cultural spheres. Local law enforcement practices underwent significant changes. The case highlighted the need for more rigorous investigative techniques and better coordination among agencies. Lessons learned from the trial influenced procedures, ensuring that future investigations would be more thorough and less susceptible to manipulation. The community of La Porte was forever altered. The trial left a scar on its collective psyche, a reminder of the darkness that had once lurked in their midst. Efforts to rebuild trust and restore normalcy were ongoing, but the shadow of Belle Gunness's crimes loomed large.

Culturally, the trial secured its place in true crime history. It became a touchstone for discussions about female criminality and the societal factors that contribute to such extreme behaviors. The story of Belle Gunness and Ray Lamphere was recounted in books, documentaries, and articles, each retelling adding to the legend. The trial's legacy was not just in the legal precedents it set but in the way it shaped the public's understanding of crime and justice. The fascination with Belle's story endured, a testament to the complex interplay of fear, intrigue, and the human capacity for darkness.

As the dust settled on the trial, the community of La Porte began to pick up the pieces, grappling with the legacy of one of America's most notorious criminals. The trial of Ray Lamphere may have concluded, but the story of Belle Gunness was far from over. The next chapter will delve into the mystery of Belle's death, exploring the theories and enduring questions that continue to captivate those drawn to her dark tale.

CHAPTER 9
THE MYSTERY OF BELLE'S DEATH

The air was thick with the smell of smoke and charred wood as the ruins of Belle Gunness's farmhouse smoldered in the early morning light. The scene was chaotic, with neighbors and local authorities milling about, their faces etched with shock and horror. As they sifted through the blackened remains, a grim discovery awaited them. Hidden beneath the debris lay the bodies of Belle's children, and amidst them, a headless, charred figure believed to be Belle herself. This initial discovery sent waves of disbelief through the community as the true extent of the horror began to unfold.

THE BURNED BODY

The initial discovery of the burned body was both a revelation and a mystery. The charred remains were virtually unrecognizable, making the task of identification a daunting one. Local authorities, led by Sheriff Smutzer, were called to the scene to oversee the grim task of sifting through the ruins. The headless body, found near the remains of Belle's children, was immediately assumed to be Belle Gunness. This assumption was based on the proximity of the body to the children and the context of the fire, which seemed to be a tragic accident at first glance. However, the condition of the body—severely burned and missing its head—complicated matters significantly.

The chaos of that morning left the community in disbelief, with speculation swirling about the fire's origins and the identity of the burned body. Neighbors whispered about Belle's fate, while some looked on in grim silence, trying to process the horrifying possibility that a woman many had considered a local fixture could be at the heart of something far darker than they had imagined. The discovery of a headless body only deepened the mystery, sparking rumors that something more sinister was at play.

The discrepancies in identifying the body soon became apparent. Belle Gunness was known to be a formidable woman, standing around six feet tall and weighing over 200 pounds. The charred body, however, did not match these physical characteristics. It appeared smaller and lighter, raising immediate questions about its true identity. The lack of definitive dental records further complicated the identification process. In the early 20th century, forensic techniques were rudimentary, and dental records were not as meticulously kept as they are today. This lack of concrete evidence left a significant gap in the investigation.

Without the forensic tools available today, investigators were left to rely on rudimentary methods to piece together the truth. The absence of definitive dental records was a critical obstacle, as dental identification was one of the few reliable techniques for identifying remains at the time. The uncertainty surrounding the body's identity fed into the growing speculation that Belle Gunness had orchestrated her own disappearance, a theory that gained traction as the investigation dragged on without clear answers.

Eyewitness testimonies added another layer of complexity. Several neighbors and acquaintances began to voice their doubts, noting that the body seemed too small to be Belle's. Some even suggested that the body might belong to another woman entirely, perhaps a housekeeper or an unfortunate visitor. These conflicting accounts created an atmosphere of uncertainty and suspicion, casting doubt on the initial identification of the body as Belle Gunness.

Adding to the confusion were accounts from individuals who had interacted with Belle in the days leading up to the fire. One neighbor mentioned seeing Belle conducting business as usual just the day before the blaze, her demeanor calm and controlled. These recollections fueled suspicions that Belle had not been caught unaware by a tragic accident, but rather that she had engineered the event with precision, using the chaos to mask her escape. The headless state of the body was particularly unsettling, raising questions about whether it had been intentionally mutilated to obscure the truth.

The autopsy and forensic analysis conducted on the body revealed further ambiguities. Dr. J. Meyer, the local coroner, performed an autopsy in an attempt to uncover more details. The examination of the bone structure suggested that the body was indeed smaller than Belle's known measurements. Dental remains, though limited, did not conclusively match Belle's dental records. Additionally, the analysis of personal items found with the body, such as jewelry and clothing, provided little to no concrete evidence. The forensic limitations of the time meant that many questions remained unanswered, and the true identity of the burned body continued to elude investigators.

The uncertainty surrounding the identification of the body had a profound impact on the investigation. The continued search for Belle Gunness became a priority for law enforcement. Sheriff Smutzer and his team were under immense pressure to provide answers to a community reeling from the revelations. The media, ever eager for sensational stories, fueled speculation and rumors. Newspapers across the country ran headlines questioning whether Belle had truly perished in the fire or if she had orchestrated an elaborate escape. This media frenzy only served to deepen the mystery, with theories ranging from the plausible to the absurd.

Law enforcement faced significant challenges in closing the case. The lack of definitive evidence meant that the investigation remained open-ended, with no clear resolution in sight. The possibility that Belle Gunness had faked her death and escaped added a layer of complexity that investigators struggled to navigate. Every lead, every piece of evidence, was scrutinized, but concrete answers remained elusive. The community of La Porte was left in a state of limbo, grappling with the uncertainty and the chilling possibility that Belle Gunness was still out there, somewhere.

ESCAPE THEORIES

The theory that Belle Gunness staged her own death to escape justice has fascinated true crime enthusiasts for over a century. The motive behind such a drastic move seems clear: avoiding capture and continuing her criminal activities. Belle was no stranger to deception and had a history of evading the law. The fire that consumed her farmhouse and the discovery of a headless body, initially presumed to be hers, created the perfect cover for escape. The condition of the body, smaller and lighter than Belle, suggested a staged scene. Some investigators believed Belle orchestrated the entire event to fake her death and disappear.

Evidence suggesting a staged scene began to surface as authorities delved deeper into the case. The meticulous planning evident in Belle's previous crimes hinted that she could have orchestrated her own "death." For instance, the headless body found in the ruins lacked the physical characteristics that matched Belle's known stature. Eyewitnesses reported seeing Belle in the days leading up to the fire, suggesting she was in control of her surroundings. Some speculated that Belle might have had accomplices who helped her execute the plan. Ray Lamphere, her former farmhand and lover, was an obvious suspect. His intimate knowledge of the farm and Belle's operations made him a likely candidate to assist in her escape, willingly or under duress.

Her ability to manage every aspect of her crimes, from luring victims to disposing of their bodies, suggested that Belle was more than capable of faking her own death. Some investigators began to wonder whether the fire was just the final act in a carefully scripted plan, one that allowed Belle to walk away from her life of murder without facing justice. Her history of deception, including the use of false identities, bolstered this theory. It wasn't beyond the realm of possibility that Belle had recruited an unwitting accomplice or even another victim to serve as her decoy in the burned remains.

Planned disappearance theories add another layer to the mystery. Belle was known for her cunning and ability to think several steps ahead. It's plausible that she meticulously planned her disappearance well in advance. Financial preparations were evident in her actions leading up to the fire. Belle was seen liquidating assets and securing funds, ensuring she had the financial means to start anew. She was also known to use disguises and false identities, making it easier for her to blend in and avoid detection. Potential escape routes and destinations were numerous, given her knowledge of the Midwest and her connections within the immigrant community.

Witness accounts and leads further fuel the escape theories. Several sightings of Belle were reported in neighboring towns shortly after the fire. These accounts described a woman matching Belle's appearance, often seen in the company of a man or traveling alone. Testimonies from individuals claiming to have assisted her added credibility to these sightings. One such account came from a local store owner who claimed to have sold provisions to a woman resembling Belle just days after the fire. Additionally, unexplained movements of Belle's finances and belongings suggested she was preparing for a life on the run. Bank records indicated withdrawals and transfers that could not be easily explained, hinting at a larger plan in motion.

One particularly intriguing sighting came from a train conductor in Chicago, who claimed to have seen a woman fitting Belle's description boarding a westbound train just days after the fire. According to his account, the woman was traveling with a large trunk, her face partially obscured by a hat and veil. The conductor's story was just one of many that stoked the public's fascination with the idea that Belle had successfully vanished into thin air, escaping both the authorities and her grim past.

Investigators faced significant challenges in proving Belle's successful escape. The lack of concrete evidence made it difficult to conclude she had eluded capture definitively. Discrepancies in witness testimonies further complicated matters, as not all accounts could be verified. Some sightings were dismissed as cases of mistaken identity, while others lacked sufficient detail to be credible. The difficulty in tracing Belle's movements post-disappearance added to the frustration. Without modern forensic techniques, tracking someone who had meticulously planned their escape was nearly impossible. The layers of deception Belle employed ensured that she remained one step ahead of those pursuing her.

The combination of these factors creates a compelling narrative that Belle Gunness, the infamous La Porte serial killer, may have indeed staged her own death and vanished into the shadows. The lack of a definitive conclusion continues to intrigue those who study her case. Belle's story is a chilling reminder of how societal and forensic limitations of the early 20th century allowed one of history's most cunning criminals to escape justice potentially. The mystery of her fate remains one of the most enduring and tantalizing questions in true crime history, inviting endless speculation and investigation.

SIGHTINGS AND RUMORS

In the weeks and months following the fire that razed Belle Gunness's farmhouse, reports of sightings began to trickle in, each one adding a layer of intrigue to the already sensational story. These early sightings were concentrated in neighboring towns and cities, where people claimed to have seen a woman matching Belle's description. She was often described as tall, with a sturdy build and a distinctive presence. In some accounts, she wore simple, unassuming clothing, likely to avoid drawing attention. The reliability of these sightings varied. Some came from credible sources, such as local shopkeepers and town officials, while others were from individuals with less verifiable backgrounds. Each report was scrutinized by law enforcement, but the absence of concrete evidence made it difficult to confirm any of the claims.

As time passed, the rumors surrounding Belle's fate only grew more elaborate. Long-term rumors suggested that Belle had assumed a new identity and was living quietly under an assumed name. There were reports of encounters with a woman fitting Belle's description in distant states and even other countries. These stories painted a picture of a fugitive constantly on the move, always one step ahead of those who pursued her. The impact of these rumors on the legend of Belle Gunness was profound. They fueled the public's fascination with her story, transforming her from a local criminal into a figure of almost mythical proportions. The idea that she had outwitted the authorities and escaped justice captured the imagination of many, ensuring her place in true crime lore.

Belle's story became a symbol of defiance and cunning, particularly in an era when women were expected to be passive and obedient. Her ability to evade capture and manipulate those around her defied the gender norms of the time, adding an extra layer of intrigue to her story. For many, the possibility that she had escaped into a new life, free from the consequences of her heinous acts, was both terrifying and captivating. It was this combination of audacity and mystery that cemented Belle's place in the annals of true crime, ensuring that her story would be told and retold for generations.

High-profile claims further stoked the flames of speculation. Some of the victims' families, desperate for closure, hired private investigators to track down leads. These investigators often found themselves navigating a web of half-truths and dead ends, but their efforts kept the case in the public eye. Media-driven investigations and exposés added another layer of complexity. Journalists eager for a sensational story conducted their own inquiries, sometimes uncovering new leads, but more often than not, they perpetuated the mystery. Law enforcement's response to these high-profile claims was cautious. While they could not ignore the possibility that Belle had escaped, the lack of concrete evidence made it difficult to take definitive action. Each lead was investigated thoroughly, but the elusive nature of the truth made it hard to draw any solid conclusions.

Public fascination with Belle's potential escape played a significant role in keeping the rumors alive. Sensationalist media coverage was a driving force behind this. Newspapers and magazines ran stories with eye-catching headlines, speculating on Belle's whereabouts and presenting the latest unverified sightings as fact. This coverage captivated true crime enthusiasts and amateur sleuths, who were drawn to the mystery and the challenge of piecing together the clues. The cultural impact of Belle's enigmatic end was considerable. She became a symbol of defiance against societal norms, a woman who had not only committed heinous crimes but had also managed to slip through the fingers of justice. Her story was retold in books, articles, and even plays, each iteration adding to her legend and ensuring that her name would not be forgotten.

The role of true crime enthusiasts and amateur sleuths in perpetuating the rumors cannot be underestimated. These individuals, driven by a mix of curiosity and a desire for justice, delved into the details of Belle's case with an almost obsessive fervor. They pored over old newspaper clippings, interviewed surviving relatives of the victims, and even visited the sites connected to Belle's life and crimes. Their efforts, while often speculative, kept the investigation alive in the public consciousness. The cultural fascination with Belle's story extended beyond the realm of true crime aficionados. Her tale resonated with those interested in the psychological complexities of criminal behavior and the societal factors that shape such actions. Belle's ability to defy expectations and evade capture made her a compelling figure, one whose story continues to intrigue and confound to this day.

MODERN INVESTIGATIONS

Decades after Belle Gunness's farmhouse was reduced to ashes, the mystery of her fate continued to captivate the public imagination. With the advent of modern forensic science, efforts to reopen and reexamine her case gained momentum. Forensic experts, equipped with advanced technology, embarked on a quest to uncover the truth. They collaborated with historians and delved into archives, piecing together clues that had long lain dormant.

With advancements in DNA technology, investigators began revisiting cold cases like Belle Gunness's, hoping that modern science could solve what had been impossible in the early 1900s. New techniques, such as mitochondrial DNA analysis, offered the possibility of identifying even degraded remains, prompting renewed efforts to match Belle's descendants with the burned body. However, the condition of the remains, along with the lack of viable tissue samples, proved to be significant hurdles in definitively closing the case.

In recent years, a significant push has come from DNA analysis attempts aimed at confirming the identity of the burned body found in the ruins. Investigators collected DNA samples from possible descendants of Belle Gunness. Comparisons were made with the remains found at the crime scene, but the process was fraught with challenges. The samples from the early 1900s were often degraded, making it difficult to extract viable DNA. Despite these obstacles, the pursuit continued, driven by the hope that modern science could finally resolve the century-old mystery.

New findings and revelations emerged as modern investigations progressed. The reanalysis of old evidence using cutting-edge techniques provided fresh insights. For instance, forensic experts uncovered new leads by examining artifacts and documents previously overlooked. Advanced imaging technologies, such as 3D scanning of skeletal remains, offered a more detailed understanding of the physical characteristics of the burned body. These technological advancements deepened the understanding of Belle Gunness's activities and the extent of her crimes, shedding new light on her possible fate.

Current theories about Belle Gunness's fate, based on modern investigations, reflect a blend of consensus and unanswered questions. Many forensic experts and historians agree that the burned body found in the farmhouse was not Belle's, supporting the theory that she faked her death. However, the exact details of her escape and subsequent life remain elusive. Persistent unanswered questions fuel ongoing interest in the case. Public fascination with Belle Gunness endures as both amateur sleuths and academic researchers continue to explore the depths of her story. The case of Belle Gunness remains a compelling example of how modern forensic science can breathe new life into historical mysteries.

In the next chapter, we will delve into the psychological profile of Belle Gunness. By examining her mental state through the lens of modern psychology, we aim to understand the mind behind the murders and what drove her to commit such heinous acts.

CHAPTER 10
PSYCHOLOGICAL PROFILE

The foggy mornings of Norway, with their eerie stillness, might have seemed like an unending canvas of gray to young Brynhild Paulsdatter Storset, known later as Belle Gunness. Yet, behind her calm demeanor, there simmered a darkness that would one day consume the lives of many. Understanding Belle's psychological profile requires us to peer into the shadows of her early life, where the seeds of her later monstrous deeds were sown.

Raised in the rugged and unforgiving Norwegian countryside, Belle's early life was far from idyllic. The harsh realities of farm life, combined with the rigid societal structures of 19th-century Norway, would have created an environment where Belle's emerging personality traits could have been easily masked by the expectations placed upon her as a young girl. But even in these early years, those who knew her sensed that beneath the surface lurked a cold and calculating mind.

EARLY PSYCHOLOGICAL SIGNS

Belle's childhood behavior hinted at the psychological complexities that would later define her. From a young age, she exhibited a disturbing propensity for cruelty. Stories from her early years describe instances where she took pleasure in inflicting pain on animals, a common early indicator of more severe antisocial behavior. This cruelty was not limited to animals. Belle often manipulated and deceived other children, showcasing an alarming lack of empathy. One tale recounts how she tricked a neighborhood child into eating spoiled food, watching with detached curiosity as the child fell ill. These early displays of manipulation and deceit were harbingers of the cold, calculating nature she would later perfect.

Though outwardly Belle appeared as just another child of her time, it was clear to those closest to her that she harbored a darker nature. Accounts from her family and village suggest that Belle's cruelty, while unsettling, was often dismissed or ignored, seen as an eccentricity rather than an indicator of more serious psychological issues. In a small, insular community, such behaviors could easily slip through the cracks, allowing Belle to further hone her manipulative tendencies without the interference of external authorities.

As Belle transitioned into adolescence, her behavior evolved in more troubling ways. She became increasingly rebellious, clashing with authority figures and displaying a marked disregard for societal norms. Her actions grew more antisocial, aligning with the early signs of thrill-seeking behavior. Belle seemed to derive a perverse satisfaction from taking risks and defying expectations. This period of her life was characterized by strained relationships with both peers and adults. She was known to challenge teachers and elders, pushing boundaries and testing limits. These interactions highlighted her emerging pattern of seeking control and dominance, traits that would become central to her criminal persona.

As Belle entered adulthood, these traits became more pronounced, especially in her relationships with men. In a world where women were expected to be subservient and docile, Belle stood out for her refusal to adhere to these norms. She seemed to revel in the power she held over others, particularly men, and began to exploit societal expectations of femininity to her advantage. This marked the beginning of a long history of deception and manipulation that would ultimately lead to murder.

The dynamics within Belle's family played a pivotal role in shaping her psychological development. Her father, Paul Pedersen Storset, was a strict and demanding man whose methods of discipline were often harsh. The fear and obedience he instilled in his children created an environment where Belle learned to navigate power dynamics. Her interactions with her siblings were equally influential. Competition for their father's approval fostered sibling rivalry, with Belle often emerging as the dominant force. These early familial conflicts honed her manipulative skills and reinforced her desire for control. The family's financial hardships added another layer of stress, fueling Belle's ambitions and driving her towards increasingly ruthless behavior.

Belle's interactions with her community further illustrate her complex psychological profile. In the tight-knit environment of her Norwegian village, she was known for her unusual and often concerning behavior. Neighbors whispered about her odd demeanor and the unsettling incidents that seemed to follow her. Reports of early criminal activities, such as petty theft and deceit, began to surface. These actions, though minor at the time, were indicative of Belle's growing disregard for moral and legal boundaries. Her reputation within the community was a mix of fear and fascination, with many recognizing the darkness that lurked beneath her outward charm.

The psychological landscape of Belle Gunness is a tapestry woven from early experiences of cruelty, manipulation, and a profound lack of empathy. Her childhood and adolescent behavior, shaped by familial and community dynamics, set her on a path of escalating violence and deception. As you delve deeper into her story, consider how these early signs of psychological disturbance foreshadowed the monstrous acts that would later define her life. Belle's tale is not just one of crime and horror but a window into the complexities of the human psyche and the factors that can drive a person to such extremes.

NARCISSISM AND PSYCHOPATHY

Belle Gunness, known for her charm and manipulative prowess, displayed numerous traits of narcissism throughout her life. Her grandiose sense of self-importance was evident in her interactions and the way she presented herself. Belle believed she deserved wealth and admiration, often portraying herself as a virtuous widow deserving of sympathy and support. This sense of entitlement drove many of her actions, from placing matrimonial ads to luring wealthy suitors to her farm. She thrived on admiration and attention, carefully crafting her public image to elicit favorable responses from those around her. This need for validation was not just a superficial desire but a core aspect of her personality that fueled her manipulative schemes.

Belle's relationships were deeply exploitative, with her using charm and deceit to get what she wanted. A case study of her manipulation of men reveals how she exploited societal expectations of women to her advantage. In her personal ads, Belle painted herself as a loving and devoted woman seeking companionship. This facade played into the societal belief that women were nurturing and trustworthy. Once her suitors arrived, she lavished them with attention and affection, creating an illusion of genuine interest. However, her true intentions were far darker. She used these men for financial gain, promising love and security while plotting their demise. This manipulation extended to the point of convincing them to bring large sums of money, which she promptly took before ending their lives.

Belle's ability to manipulate the expectations of those around her was crucial to her success as a serial killer. By projecting an image of the perfect widow and mother, she disarmed her victims, convincing them of her innocence and dependability. This manipulation of societal norms—her calculated use of her gender as a shield—allowed her to continue her crimes for years without suspicion. The men who came into her life were taken in by her charm and never suspected the dark fate that awaited them.

Psychopathy, another significant aspect of Belle's psychological profile, was marked by a chilling lack of empathy and remorse. Belle's charm was superficial, a tool she wielded with precision. Her ability to appear warm and caring was a stark contrast to the cold-heartedness she exhibited behind closed doors. This superficial charm allowed her to deceive not only her victims but also the community, who saw her as a respectable widow. Belle's impulsivity and poor behavioral controls were evident in her erratic actions and the risks she took. Despite the calculated nature of her murders, there were moments where her impulsiveness led to sloppy mistakes, such as leaving behind incriminating evidence.

Several case studies highlight Belle's psychopathic traits in specific incidents. Her manipulative interactions with suitors often began with letters filled with promises and flattery. Once they arrived, she would isolate them from their families, ensuring no one would come looking for them. Her callous treatment of victims before and after their deaths was particularly disturbing. Belle showed no hesitation in using brutal methods to end their lives, from poisoning to bludgeoning. Her deceptive behavior extended to authorities and community members. When questioned about the whereabouts of her suitors, she provided plausible explanations, often using fake letters to suggest they had moved on or met with unfortunate accidents.

Comparing Belle's behavior to other known psychopaths, both male and female, reveals striking similarities. Like male serial killers such as Dennis Rader and Ted Bundy, Belle exhibited no outward signs of remorse for her crimes. Her methods were brutal and efficient, reflecting a complete disregard for human life. Female psychopaths, like Aileen Wuornos, also displayed similar traits of manipulation and superficial charm. Belle's criminal methods and psychological profile align closely with these individuals, though her motivations and execution of crimes had distinct nuances. While male psychopaths often seek power and control, Belle's actions were driven by financial gain and a desire to maintain her facade of respectability.

In understanding Belle Gunness, you see the confluence of narcissism and psychopathy, creating a complex and dangerous individual. Her grandiose sense of self, need for admiration, and exploitative relationships were intertwined with a lack of empathy, superficial charm, and impulsive behavior. These traits allowed her to manipulate and deceive with chilling efficiency, leaving a trail of victims in her wake. Belle's story offers a profound insight into the mind of a female psychopath, challenging traditional notions and expanding our understanding of criminal psychology.

FINANCIAL MOTIVATIONS

Belle Gunness's life was marked by an unrelenting pursuit of financial stability, a drive deeply rooted in her economic background. Growing up in the harsh landscapes of rural Norway, Belle experienced poverty firsthand. Her family's financial struggles left an indelible mark on her psyche. The scarcity of resources meant every penny was hard-earned, and the constant pressure to make ends meet was a daily reality. This environment of deprivation and economic instability planted the seeds of Belle's obsession with wealth. When she immigrated to the United States, she carried these financial anxieties with her. The journey to a new land, filled with the promise of prosperity, was also fraught with uncertainty and stress. Upon arriving in the U.S., Belle faced immediate financial challenges. Finding work was difficult, and the jobs she secured offered meager wages, insufficient to meet her aspirations. The financial pressures of her immigrant experience further fueled her desire for economic security and drove her to seek out more lucrative—and ultimately nefarious—opportunities.

Belle's opportunistic approach to finance was evident in her use of marriage and relationships for financial gain. She viewed her suitors not as partners but as stepping stones to wealth. Belle's first husband, Mads Sorenson, fell victim to this ruthless strategy. She convinced him to take out multiple life insurance policies, ensuring a substantial payout upon his untimely death. The overlapping policies were no accident; they were a calculated move to maximize financial gain. Belle's second husband, Peter Gunness, met a similar fate. The insurance money from these marriages funded her subsequent ventures, allowing her to invest in property and other assets. Belle's penchant for insurance fraud extended beyond her husbands. She placed personal ads to lure wealthy men to her farm, where they met gruesome ends. Each victim was carefully selected for their financial resources, and Belle wasted no time in securing their assets. The money she obtained through these schemes was invested in various ventures, including real estate, which provided a steady stream of income. Belle's financial opportunism was relentless, and her ability to exploit relationships for monetary gain was both chilling and efficient.

Her cunning financial schemes extended beyond simple theft. Belle meticulously calculated the timing of her crimes, ensuring that her victims had cut off contact with their families before they disappeared. By isolating them, she eliminated any chance that someone might come looking for them too soon, giving her the time she needed to liquidate their assets and cover her tracks. In many cases, she even convinced her victims to update their wills, ensuring that she would be the primary beneficiary.

Patterns in Belle's financial crimes reveal a clear escalation over time. Her early fraudulent activities were relatively small-scale, such as inflating the value of lost or damaged property to collect larger insurance payouts. These initial scams were testing grounds for her more elaborate schemes. As Belle's confidence grew, so did the scale of her crimes. She transitioned from petty theft and minor fraud to sophisticated and large-scale operations. The personal ads she placed were part of a well-oiled machine designed to attract and trap wealthy victims. Each scheme was meticulously planned to ensure maximum financial gain with minimal risk. Belle's focus on monetary gain was unwavering. Every action, every murder, was a means to an end—accumulating wealth. Her criminal activities were characterized by a consistent and singular focus on financial success. This relentless pursuit of money drove her to commit increasingly heinous acts, each more calculated than the last.

The psychological drive behind Belle's pursuit of wealth was deeply intertwined with her sense of self-worth. For Belle, financial success was not just a means of survival; it was a measure of her value as a person. Growing up in poverty had instilled in her a profound fear of economic instability. Accumulating wealth became a way to exert control over her life and circumstances. Money provided Belle with power and security, allowing her to manipulate her surroundings and the people in it. This sense of control was intoxicating, feeding into her narcissistic tendencies. Belle derived emotional satisfaction from financial manipulation. Each successful scheme, each insurance payout, was a validation of her cunning and intelligence. The thrill of outsmarting her victims and authorities alike provided a perverse sense of accomplishment. Belle's pursuit of wealth was not merely about the money itself but about what it represented—power, control, and a sense of superiority over those who fell prey to her schemes.

For Belle, wealth was not just a means of survival; it was a testament to her superiority over others. She took a perverse pride in outsmarting the men who fell into her traps, relishing the power she held over them. In her mind, each financial conquest was proof that she was smarter, more resourceful, and more deserving of success than anyone else. This belief in her own superiority, coupled with her lack of empathy, allowed her to rationalize her actions and continue her killing spree without guilt.

EXPERT ANALYSIS AND DIAGNOSES

Forensic psychologists have long been fascinated by Belle Gunness, whose actions defy simple explanations. Diagnosing specific disorders like Antisocial Personality Disorder (ASPD) involves examining a pattern of behaviors that align with established criteria. Belle's life offers a textbook case of ASPD. She exhibited a pervasive disregard for the rights of others, as seen in her willingness to manipulate, deceive, and murder without remorse. Her behaviors included lying, conning others for personal profit, and showing a lack of empathy, all hallmarks of this disorder. Psychological assessments of her actions reveal a chilling consistency in her methods, indicating a deeply ingrained pathology. Experts suggest that her motivations were multifaceted, driven by a combination of financial greed, a desire for control, and a need to maintain her facade of respectability. Belle's mental state was marked by a profound detachment from the suffering she inflicted, allowing her to carry out her crimes with cold efficiency.

Belle's case challenges traditional views of female serial killers, who are often characterized as acting out of revenge or mental instability. Instead, Belle's crimes were coldly calculated, driven by a relentless desire for wealth and power. This sets her apart from many of her contemporaries, both male and female, and has led modern psychologists to reevaluate the role of gender in criminal behavior. Belle's ability to blend into society while committing such heinous acts underscores the complexity of her psychological profile.

Understanding Belle's behavior requires a historical context. In the early 1900s, psychological understanding was rudimentary compared to today's standards. Female criminality was often misunderstood, with societal norms influencing diagnoses. Women who committed crimes were frequently seen through a lens of hysteria or moral deficiency rather than complex psychological disorders. Modern criteria for diagnosing personality disorders provide a clearer framework, emphasizing patterns of behavior over isolated incidents. Today, Belle would likely be diagnosed with ASPD, characterized by persistent antisocial behavior, deceit, and a lack of remorse. This evolution in psychological understanding highlights the importance of context in interpreting criminal behavior. Historical views often lacked the nuance to fully capture the complexities of individuals like Belle, who defied societal norms in profoundly disturbing ways.

In interviews with modern experts in criminal psychology and forensic psychiatry, Belle's psychological profile is dissected with the benefit of contemporary knowledge. Dr. J. Reid Meloy, a renowned forensic psychologist, explains that Belle's combination of charm, manipulation, and brutality aligns with traits seen in psychopathic serial killers. Comparing her to contemporary female serial killers, experts note similarities in methods and motivations. However, the challenge of posthumous diagnosis remains significant. Without the ability to conduct direct assessments, experts must rely on historical records and behavioral patterns, making definitive conclusions difficult. This challenge underscores the complexity of diagnosing historical figures, where context and available evidence play crucial roles.

Despite these challenges, modern forensic psychologists agree that Belle Gunness exhibited many of the hallmark traits of both narcissistic personality disorder and psychopathy. Her lack of empathy, her grandiose sense of self-worth, and her ability to charm and manipulate those around her align closely with the diagnostic criteria for these disorders. While it is impossible to make a definitive diagnosis without direct examination, the patterns of behavior she displayed throughout her life strongly suggest a combination of these two personality disorders.

Belle's case has profoundly influenced modern criminal profiling and psychological analysis. Her actions contributed to a deeper understanding of female serial killers, who were often overlooked in early psychological studies. Lessons learned from Belle's profile emphasize the importance of recognizing patterns of manipulation and deceit, traits that are not always immediately apparent. Her case has also influenced investigative techniques, encouraging a more nuanced approach to profiling female offenders. By examining Belle's life, modern profilers have gained insights into the psychological makeup of female serial killers, enhancing their ability to identify and apprehend such individuals. These contributions have shaped the field, highlighting the need for comprehensive and context-aware analyses in understanding criminal behavior.

As we conclude this exploration of Belle Gunness's psychological profile, we see a complex interplay of factors that shaped her actions. Her diagnoses, influenced by both historical and modern perspectives, paint a picture of a deeply disturbed individual driven by a mix of greed, control, and detachment. The insights gained from her case continue to inform our understanding of female criminality, offering valuable lessons for both psychological analysis and criminal profiling.

CHAPTER 11
COMPARATIVE ANALYSIS

The swirling fog and the eerie silence of early 20th-century America set the stage for some of the most notorious figures in criminal history. Among them, H.H. Holmes stands out, a name synonymous with cunning and cruelty. Just as we explore Belle Gunness's dark deeds, Holmes's legacy offers another chilling glimpse into the depths of human depravity. His "Murder Castle" in Chicago became an architectural embodiment of his twisted mind, a labyrinthine structure designed to facilitate murder and concealment.

The design of the 'Murder Castle' was a testament to Holmes's meticulous planning and his cold detachment from human life. The sheer complexity of the structure, with its secret hallways and soundproofed rooms, reflected a mind that not only relished murder but sought to make it a routine operation. In contrast, Belle Gunness's methods were simpler, more straightforward. Where Holmes created a sprawling deathtrap, Belle used her home as a lure, presenting it as a sanctuary of love and domestic bliss. The psychological nuances in their approaches reveal much about their respective desires for control and manipulation.

H. H. HOLMES

H.H. Holmes, born Herman Webster Mudgett in New Hampshire in 1861, was a man of many faces. He moved to Illinois in 1885, abandoning his wife and child, and adopted the name Holmes. He initially worked at a pharmacy near Jackson Park, the future site of the 1893 World's Fair. It was during this period that he began constructing what would become the infamous "Murder Castle" in the Englewood neighborhood of Chicago. This seemingly ordinary building was anything but. Designed with secret passageways, trapdoors, soundproof rooms, and a basement equipped with acid vats, quicklime pits, and a crematorium, the "Murder Castle" was a house of horrors. Holmes lured victims, primarily women, with promises of employment or lodging, only to lead them to their deaths within the castle's nightmarish confines.

Holmes's victims, much like Belle's, were drawn in by a false sense of security. The World's Fair, with its promises of progress and modernity, became the perfect backdrop for his heinous activities. Many of his victims were young women seeking new opportunities in the bustling city, unaware of the dangers that awaited them. Holmes, like Belle, played on the vulnerabilities of his victims, using charm and deception to disarm them before their brutal demise.

Holmes's methods of murder were as varied as they were macabre. Much like Belle, he used deception and charm to attract his victims. However, while Belle focused on financial gain, Holmes often seemed driven by a sadistic thrill. He employed a range of killing methods, including poisoning, suffocation, and dismemberment. Victims were often trapped in airtight rooms, where they would be asphyxiated or led into chambers that led directly to the basement, where their bodies met more gruesome ends. Holmes's disposal of bodies echoed Belle's methods in its meticulousness. He used acid vats to dissolve corpses and quicklime pits to hasten decomposition, ensuring that little trace of his victims remained.

When comparing the psychological profiles of Holmes and Gunness, the similarities are striking yet nuanced. Both exhibited clear narcissistic and psychopathic traits. They were manipulative, charming, and displayed a complete lack of empathy for their victims. However, their motivations diverged. Belle's crimes were primarily financially motivated. She sought wealth and stability, using marriage and promises of love as tools to secure her victims' assets. Holmes, on the other hand, appeared to derive a sadistic pleasure from his acts. While financial gain was a factor, the thrill of the kill and the elaborate nature of his murders suggested a deeper, more intrinsic drive for power and control. Both Holmes and Gunness were adept at manipulating those around them, creating facades of respectability that masked their true natures. Yet, Holmes's elaborate "Murder Castle" and his penchant for theatrics highlighted a more pronounced desire for psychological dominance.

The impact and legacy of H.H. Holmes and Belle Gunness in popular culture and public consciousness reveal the enduring fascination with their crimes. Holmes's capture and trial garnered immense media attention, turning him into a figure of macabre curiosity. His story was sensationalized in newspapers, much like Belle's, feeding the public's morbid fascination with his deeds. Holmes's infamy has persisted over the years, immortalized in literature and film, most notably in Erik Larson's "The Devil in the White City." His "Murder Castle" became a symbol of the hidden horrors lurking beneath the veneer of urban progress, much like Belle's farm symbolized the darkness that could exist in the rural heartland.

In comparing their legacies, it is evident that both Holmes and Gunness have left indelible marks on true crime literature and media. Their stories continue to captivate and horrify, serving as grim reminders of the depths of human cruelty. The public reaction to their crimes was one of shock and disbelief, amplified by the sensationalized media coverage that surrounded their cases. This coverage not only fed public curiosity but also cemented their places in the annals of criminal history. Their tales have influenced countless works of fiction and non-fiction, shaping the way we understand and engage with the concept of the serial killer.

In exploring the stories of H.H. Holmes and Belle Gunness, you are compelled to confront the uncomfortable truths about human nature and the societal conditions that allow such darkness to flourish. These cases challenge our perceptions of safety and trust, revealing how easily charisma and charm can mask malevolence. As you delve deeper into their lives, you are reminded of the thin line between civilization and savagery and the enduring allure of the macabre.

JANE TOPPAN

Jane Toppan, born Honora Kelley in 1857, had a life marred by early trauma and instability. Her mother died of tuberculosis when she was young, and her father, known as "Kelley the Crack," was rumored to have stitched his own eyelids together. This unstable environment led to her being placed in the Boston Female Asylum, an orphanage, in 1863. She was later adopted by Mrs. Ann C. Toppan in Lowell, Massachusetts, where she was renamed Jane Toppan. Jane's early life was a mix of hardship and adaptation, shaping her into a complex individual who masked her inner turmoil with an outwardly pleasant demeanor.

The trauma of Jane's early years, combined with the instability of her family life, laid the foundation for the psychological disturbances that would later manifest in her murderous actions. Much like Belle Gunness, Jane's ability to mask her true intentions behind a veneer of normalcy allowed her to operate undetected for years. This duality—presenting one face to the world while hiding another—was a key factor in both women's success as serial killers.

Jane pursued a career in nursing, entering training at Cambridge Hospital in 1885. Her access to vulnerable patients provided the perfect cover for her dark inclinations. Jane began experimenting with morphine and atropine on her patients, administering these poisons under the guise of medical treatment. Unlike Belle Gunness, who sought financial gain, Jane found pleasure in the act of killing itself. She often administered small doses of poison to bring her victims to the brink of death, then revived them, only to repeat the process. This sadistic cycle provided her with a sense of power and control, making her unique among serial killers of her time.

Jane Toppan's methods of murder were deeply intertwined with her medical knowledge. She used her position as a nurse to gain the trust of her patients, then exploited that trust to administer lethal doses of morphine and atropine. This medical expertise allowed her to disguise the true nature of her actions, making it appear as though her victims had died of natural causes. In contrast, Belle Gunness relied on more varied methods, including poisoning, blunt force, and arson, to achieve her ends. Both women used their understanding of human behavior to manipulate their victims, but Jane's methods were more clinical and detached, reflecting her background in healthcare.

Psychologically, Jane Toppan and Belle Gunness shared many traits, yet their motivations diverged significantly. Jane derived a perverse pleasure from watching her victims suffer, taking delight in their pain and the power she wielded over life and death. This sadistic pleasure set her apart from Belle, whose primary motivation was financial gain. Jane's enjoyment of the act of killing itself made her crimes particularly chilling. Both women, however, were master manipulators. They used charm and deceit to lure their victims into a false sense of security, only to betray them when they were most vulnerable. This manipulative behavior underscores a deep-seated need for control and dominance in both killers.

The impact and legacy of Jane Toppan's crimes were profound, though they played out differently from those of Belle Gunness. Jane's arrest in 1901 and subsequent trial shocked the public, not just because of the number of her victims but because she was a trusted caregiver. The media coverage of her trial emphasized her role as a nurse, heightening the sense of betrayal felt by the public. Unlike Belle, whose crimes were often viewed through the lens of her gender and immigrant status, Jane's actions were primarily framed as a violation of the trust inherent in the medical profession. This difference in perception highlights the varying ways gender and occupation can influence public reaction to crime.

Jane Toppan's legacy in the field of criminal psychology and profiling is significant. Her case provided early insights into the mind of a female serial killer, challenging the contemporary understanding of criminal behavior. Her sadistic pleasure in killing, combined with her use of medical knowledge, offered a unique profile that has influenced subsequent studies of female psychopaths. Jane's crimes forced society to confront uncomfortable truths about the potential for evil in trusted figures, a theme that continues to resonate in true crime literature and media.

Jane's case offers early insight into the concept of 'angel of mercy' killers, individuals who use their professional roles to commit crimes under the guise of caregiving. Unlike Belle, who sought to financially benefit from her murders, Jane's motivations were rooted in a need for power and control over life and death. The clinical detachment with which she administered lethal doses of poison, coupled with her ability to prolong her victims' suffering, set her apart as one of the most chilling figures in early criminal history.

As you reflect on Jane Toppan's story, consider the broader implications of her actions. How did her early life experiences shape her path? What does her case reveal about the nature of trust and betrayal in professional relationships? These questions not only deepen our understanding of Jane Toppan but also challenge us to think critically about the societal structures that can both conceal and reveal the darkest aspects of human nature.

THE AXEMAN OF NEW ORLEANS

In the sultry, jazz-filled streets of New Orleans, a figure emerged whose brutality and anonymity would forever etch his name into the annals of American crime. The Axeman of New Orleans terrorized the city between May 1918 and October 1919, leaving a trail of bloody crime scenes that baffled law enforcement and horrified the public. His weapon of choice was an ax, often taken from the very homes of his victims. The Axeman would remove a panel from the backdoor to gain entry, striking in the dead of night to unleash his savage attacks. Despite numerous attempts to capture him, the case remains unsolved, adding an eerie mystique to his legend.

The Axeman's methods were starkly brutal and seemingly random. Unlike Belle Gunness, whose murders were calculated and premeditated, the Axeman's attacks were frenzied and chaotic. He targeted Italian immigrants or Italian-Americans, leading to speculation about ethnic motivations or mafia ties, though no evidence supported these theories. Belle's killings were precise and carried out with a cold, methodical approach, often involving poison or blunt force. Her victims were lured into a false sense of security, manipulated through promises of love or prosperity. In contrast, the Axeman's victims were often attacked in their sleep, with no prior interaction or warning. His motives remain unclear, whether it was pure bloodlust, thrill-seeking, or something more sinister.

Psychologically, the Axeman and Belle Gunness present a fascinating study in contrasts. The Axeman operated under a shroud of anonymity, his identity never revealed, adding to his elusiveness. He struck fear into the hearts of New Orleans residents, his very name becoming synonymous with terror. Belle, on the other hand, maintained a public persona of a grieving widow and loving mother, using her charm and manipulation to mask her true nature. While Belle's actions were driven by a desire for financial gain and control, the Axeman's motivations appear more thrill-based, deriving pleasure from the act of killing itself. The Axeman's randomness and lack of personal connection to his victims stand in stark contrast to Belle's calculated approach, where each victim was carefully chosen and exploited.

The impact and legacy of the Axeman of New Orleans are deeply ingrained in the city's culture and folklore. Public fear reached a fever pitch during his reign of terror, exacerbated by sensationalized media coverage. Newspapers published lurid accounts of his crimes, stoking panic and speculation. One infamous letter, purportedly from the Axeman himself, threatened more murders unless jazz music was played in homes, a bizarre demand that only added to his legend. This letter, published on March 13, 1919, ensured that on the specified night, March 19, 1919, jazz filled the streets of New Orleans, and no murders occurred, cementing the Axeman's place in the city's history.

The Axeman's enduring mystery has left an indelible mark on popular culture, inspiring books, songs, and television shows. Unlike Belle Gunness, whose story has been extensively documented and analyzed, the Axeman's case remains an enigma, inviting endless speculation and theories. His ability to evade capture, despite the intense manhunt, has fueled a fascination that persists to this day. The fear he instilled in the residents of New Orleans, combined with the unresolved nature of his crimes, has made the Axeman a figure of enduring intrigue and horror.

The Axeman's elusiveness only added to the terror he inflicted on New Orleans. His ability to strike without warning, leaving behind minimal evidence, created an aura of invincibility that paralyzed the city with fear. Unlike Belle Gunness, who carefully cultivated relationships with her victims, the Axeman thrived on randomness, choosing his victims seemingly without pattern or reason. This unpredictability, combined with the brutal nature of his crimes, cemented his place as one of the most terrifying figures in American criminal lore.

GENDER COMPARISONS IN SERIAL KILLING

The chilling tales of Belle Gunness and her contemporaries reveal a stark contrast in the behaviors and methods of male and female serial killers. While both genders share a propensity for manipulation and control, the paths they take often diverge, shaped largely by societal expectations and personal motivations. Male serial killers, like Albert Fish, often "hunt" their victims, choosing strangers and using brute force or elaborate schemes to capture and kill. This predatory behavior aligns with the societal stereotype of men as hunters, a role that has been ingrained for centuries. In contrast, female serial killers, such as Belle Gunness and Lizzie Halliday, tend to "gather" their victims, often targeting those within their social or familial circles. This behavior reflects the traditional role of women as nurturers, albeit in a perverse and deadly twist.

Belle Gunness's calculated approach to murder stands in stark contrast to the more visceral and spontaneous methods employed by her male counterparts. Belle meticulously planned her crimes, using personal ads to lure wealthy suitors to her farm. Once there, she would use poison or blunt force to dispatch them, all while maintaining a facade of respectability. Male killers like Albert Fish, known for his grotesque acts of cannibalism and sadism, often acted on impulse, driven by deep-seated psychological urges. This difference in method and victim selection highlights the broader societal expectations placed on men and women. Men are expected to be aggressive and dominant, while women are often seen as caretakers, roles that can distort into violence under the right conditions.

This distortion of traditional gender roles is particularly evident in the cases of Belle Gunness and Jane Toppan. Belle, the 'Black Widow,' used her position as a wife and mother to lure victims into a sense of safety, while Jane, the 'Angel of Death,' exploited her role as a caregiver to mask her deadly intentions. Both women subverted societal expectations, using their perceived innocence as a weapon in their deadly schemes. This manipulation of gender roles adds another layer of complexity to their crimes, challenging the notion that violence and cruelty are inherently masculine traits.

Societal reactions to male and female serial killers also differ significantly. Male killers are often viewed through a lens of monstrosity, their actions attributed to inherent evil or madness. Media coverage tends to focus on the brutality of their crimes, emphasizing their physical strength and aggressive nature. Female killers, on the other hand, are often portrayed as aberrations, their actions seen as a betrayal of their nurturing roles. The media often sensationalizes their femininity, framing their crimes as acts of seduction and betrayal. This gendered narrative can obscure the true motivations behind their actions, reducing complex psychological profiles to simplistic stereotypes.

Lizzie Halliday, another notorious female killer from the same era as Belle Gunness, provides a fascinating case study. Known as "The Worst Woman on Earth," Lizzie's crimes included the murders of her two husbands and several other victims. Her methods were brutal, involving shooting and stabbing, and her motives appeared to be a mix of financial gain and sheer malice. In contrast, Albert Fish, a male contemporary, committed heinous acts of torture and cannibalism driven by deep-seated sexual fantasies and psychological disorders. These case studies illustrate the varied motivations and methods employed by male and female killers, highlighting the influence of individual psychology and societal norms.

Psychological and sociological factors play a crucial role in shaping the behaviors of male and female serial killers. Gender norms and societal expectations can influence the way these individuals express their violent tendencies. Women, often expected to be passive and nurturing, might use subtle methods like poisoning to exert control, aligning with their perceived roles. Men, on the other hand, might resort to overt violence, reflecting societal expectations of dominance and aggression. Personal trauma and mental health issues further complicate these behaviors, with many killers experiencing significant psychological distress or abuse in their formative years. Socio-economic status and cultural background also play a role, with marginalized individuals often turning to crime as a means of asserting control or escaping their circumstances.

The field of criminal profiling has evolved significantly over the years, influenced by the study of both male and female serial killers. Early profiling techniques often focused on male behaviors, leading to a gender bias in investigations. However, cases like Belle Gunness's have highlighted the need for a more nuanced approach. Modern profiling techniques now consider gender-specific behaviors, acknowledging that female killers might operate differently from their male counterparts. This evolution in profiling has led to more effective investigative methods, helping law enforcement to identify and apprehend female serial killers with greater accuracy. The contributions of cases like Belle Gunness's have been invaluable, providing insights into the complex interplay of gender, psychology, and societal influence in shaping criminal behavior.

As you reflect on the broader implications of these gender comparisons, consider how deeply societal norms and personal experiences shape human behavior. The stories of Belle Gunness, Lizzie Halliday, and Albert Fish challenge us to look beyond the surface, to understand the underlying factors that drive individuals to commit such heinous acts. These tales remind us of the complexities of the human mind and the societal structures that can both conceal and reveal the darkest aspects of our nature.

CHAPTER 12
LEGACY AND IMPACT

MEDIA LEGACY

The morning sun cast long shadows over the charred remains of Belle Gunness's farmhouse, illuminating the extent of the devastation. As investigators sifted through the ashes, the discovery of multiple bodies sent shockwaves through the community of La Porte, Indiana. The immediate media reaction was nothing short of a frenzy. Newspapers across the country seized on the gruesome details, plastering sensational headlines on their front pages. Stories bearing lurid titles like "Lured to Death by Love Letters" and "Fifteen Victims Die in Big Murder Plot" (SOURCE 1) captivated the public's imagination. The media's focus on Belle's gender and physical appearance added an extra layer of intrigue; she was often portrayed as a monstrous femme fatale, a stark contrast to the genteel widow she had presented herself as.

The rise of sensationalist journalism, often referred to as 'yellow journalism,' played a significant role in the widespread coverage of Belle's crimes. Publications like the *New York World* and the *Chicago Tribune* were quick to embellish details to capture readers' attention, drawing on the public's fascination with lurid crimes. Headlines were crafted to evoke strong emotional reactions, portraying Belle as a larger-than-life figure, capable of unimaginable cruelty. This sensationalist approach not only increased circulation but also cemented Belle's image as a cultural icon of female villainy.

The initial coverage of Belle Gunness's crimes set the tone for how she would be remembered. Newspapers were quick to emphasize her dual identity: the loving mother and the cold-hearted killer. The stark contrast between these personas was irresistible to journalists, who wove narratives that highlighted her ability to deceive and manipulate. The lurid details of her methods—poisoning, bludgeoning, and burning her victims—were recounted in graphic detail, feeding the public's morbid curiosity. This sensationalism not only sold papers but also shaped the public's perception of Belle as a uniquely dangerous woman, someone who had weaponized her femininity in the most horrifying way.

Even more striking was how the media leveraged Belle's status as an immigrant woman. The xenophobic undertones present in many reports painted her as a 'foreign menace,' playing into the fears and biases of early 20th-century America. The fact that she had come from Norway added an exotic, 'otherworldly' aspect to her crimes, allowing the media to frame her as an outsider who had infiltrated the heartland of America with sinister intent. These elements amplified the moral panic of the time, contributing to a broader narrative that criminalized immigrant communities.

Over the decades, Belle Gunness's story has proven to have remarkable staying power in the media. Her name has appeared in countless newspapers and magazines, each retelling her tale with fresh angles and new speculations. Radio and television documentaries have dissected every aspect of her life and crimes, from her early years in Norway to her mysterious disappearance. The advent of digital media has only amplified this interest, with true crime podcasts dedicating entire series to unraveling the mysteries of the Murder Farm. Belle's story continues to fascinate because it touches on so many enduring themes: the allure of the American Dream, the darkness lurking beneath a facade of respectability, and the chilling reality of a woman who defied every societal norm.

The coverage of Belle Gunness's crimes has had a lasting impact on the field of journalism itself. The early 20th century saw a shift towards sensationalism in crime reporting, a trend that was both influenced by and contributory to cases like Belle's. Journalists were eager to expose the most shocking details, often at the expense of ethical considerations. This period marked the beginning of a more tabloid-style approach to crime reporting, where the focus was on captivating the reader rather than providing a balanced account. The ethical dilemmas of covering such gruesome crimes were often overshadowed by the drive for higher circulation numbers. Yet, this sensationalism played a crucial role in shaping the public's understanding of female criminals, reinforcing stereotypes even as it brought attention to the complexities of gender and crime.

The narrative surrounding Belle Gunness has evolved significantly over time. Early portrayals painted her as a one-dimensional villain, a woman driven purely by greed and malice. However, modern interpretations have sought to understand the psychological and societal factors that may have contributed to her actions. New evidence and theories have emerged, prompting investigative journalists to revisit the case with fresh eyes. This ongoing analysis has uncovered new angles, such as the possible influence of early feminist movements on Belle's ambitions or the role of immigrant struggles in shaping her ruthless pursuit of financial security. These evolving narratives reflect a broader trend in true crime journalism, where the focus has shifted from mere sensationalism to a deeper exploration of the human psyche and societal influences.

New feminist interpretations of Belle's life propose that her story can be seen as an extreme reflection of the struggle for female autonomy in a male-dominated society. At a time when women had few legal or financial rights, Belle's actions, although horrific, can be viewed through the lens of survival in a world that afforded her few legitimate opportunities. This more nuanced analysis positions Belle not merely as a criminal but as a figure who, in her own twisted way, resisted the restrictions placed on her gender, making her both a subject of horror and a complex character for feminist critique.

As you reflect on Belle Gunness's legacy, consider how media coverage has both illuminated and obscured the truth of her life. The sensational headlines and lurid details captivated the public, but they also reinforced simplistic narratives that failed to capture the full complexity of her character. Over time, the media's portrayal of Belle has evolved, influenced by new evidence, changing societal norms, and a growing understanding of the psychological factors at play. This evolution mirrors broader shifts in journalism and public perception, highlighting the intricate dance between media representation and societal understanding. As we delve deeper into her story, we'll continue to uncover the layers of intrigue that make Belle Gunness a figure of enduring fascination.

INFLUENCE ON TRUE CRIME LITERATURE

In the wake of the chilling discoveries at Belle Gunness's farm, the appetite for true crime stories surged, driven by an audience eager for details on the gruesome events. Early true crime accounts were swift to follow. First-hand accounts and trial transcripts provided the raw material for the first wave of true crime literature. These texts often featured verbatim court proceedings, witness testimonies, and grisly descriptions of the unearthed remains. Early biographies and crime anthologies painted Belle as a monstrous figure, emphasizing her cunning and brutality. The public and critical reception of these accounts was overwhelmingly captivated; readers were both horrified and fascinated by the stark reality of her crimes.

The elements of Belle Gunness's story that make it so compelling for true crime literature are manifold. At the heart of it lies the intrigue of the unsolved mystery: Did Belle really perish in the fire, or did she escape to kill again? This unresolved question keeps readers on the edge of their seats, hungry for any new clue or theory. Belle's psychological complexity adds another layer of fascination. She wasn't just a killer; she was a master manipulator who defied societal norms at every turn. The gruesome and sensational nature of her murders—

ranging from poisoning to bludgeoning and the chilling tales of body disposal—provide the macabre details that true crime enthusiasts crave.

These elements of grisly discovery and moral complexity are the bedrock of modern true crime, a genre that thrives on exploring the darkest parts of human behavior while grappling with the psychological motivations that drive individuals like Belle Gunness. Her crimes, filled with layers of manipulation, greed, and violence, provide fertile ground for authors and scholars to question not only 'how' but 'why' she committed such acts, transforming Belle into a case study in the broader discussion of female criminality and moral deviance.

Several books and authors have notably contributed to the body of work surrounding Belle Gunness. Harold Schechter's "Hell's Princess" is one such title that has gained significant popularity. Schechter, a well-known true crime writer, delves deep into Belle's life, offering a meticulously researched and gripping narrative. Another notable work is "The Truth About Belle Gunness" by Lillian de la Torre, which provides a detailed account of Belle's crimes and the subsequent investigation. These works have not only captivated readers but have also elevated the genre, setting a high standard for true crime storytelling. They combine thorough research with compelling narratives, making the horrific story of Belle Gunness accessible and engaging.

Belle Gunness's story has profoundly influenced the broader true crime genre in several ways. Her tale has prompted shifts in narrative style and focus, moving from straightforward recounting of events to more nuanced explorations of the psychological and societal factors at play. The introduction of psychological profiling in true crime writing can be traced back to cases like Belle's, where understanding the mind of the criminal became as important as recounting their actions. This shift has enriched the genre, providing readers with deeper insights into the motivations and mental states of killers. Additionally, Belle's story has influenced the portrayal of female criminals in literature, challenging stereotypes and highlighting the complex interplay of gender and crime.

In exploring these shifts, it's clear that Belle Gunness's story has left an indelible mark on true crime literature. The genre has evolved to include more sophisticated analyses, blending factual recounting with psychological insights. This evolution not only satisfies the reader's curiosity but also educates them, providing a more comprehensive understanding of the factors that drive individuals to commit such heinous acts. The chilling details of Belle's crimes, combined with the unresolved mysteries and psychological depths, ensure that her story remains a touchstone in true crime literature, continually inspiring new generations of writers and readers alike.

BELLE GUNNESS IN POPULAR CULTURE

Film and television have long been fascinated by the dark allure of Belle Gunness's story. Early film portrayals during the silent film era were among the first to capture the public's imagination, transforming Belle's chilling tale into visual drama. These early adaptations often took creative liberties, emphasizing her role as a cunning seductress and ruthless killer. The lack of dialogue in silent films enhanced the eerie atmosphere, relying on expressive acting and stark imagery to convey the horror of her crimes. These films set the stage for later adaptations, embedding Belle's legend into the visual culture of the time.

Television has also explored Belle Gunness's story through various episodes and series dedicated to her life. Crime shows, and true crime series have dissected her methods and motivations, often blending historical facts with dramatic reenactments. Documentaries have taken a more factual approach, offering in-depth analyses of Belle's life and the forensic challenges of her time. These documentaries provide a platform for experts to discuss her psychological profile and the societal context that allowed her to operate undetected for so long. Each new adaptation brings fresh insights, keeping Belle's story alive in the public consciousness and continuing to intrigue new generations.

Television shows such as *Investigation Discovery's Deadly Women* and *Forensic Files* have dissected Belle's methods, offering both dramatized reenactments and factual breakdowns of the case. These programs tend to balance entertainment with forensic analysis, keeping viewers hooked while also explaining the investigative challenges of the time. The continuous reinvention of Belle's story on television highlights her lasting appeal as a figure of both mystery and morbidity.

Books and novels have further immortalized Belle Gunness in popular culture. Fictionalized accounts of her life often blur the lines between fact and fiction, weaving her story into broader narratives of crime and mystery. Novels inspired by Belle's life, such as "In the Garden of Spite" by Camilla Bruce, delve into her psyche, exploring the motivations and traumas that may have driven her to commit such heinous acts. These fictionalized stories allow authors to fill in the gaps left by historical records, creating compelling and immersive narratives that captivate readers. The balance between historical accuracy and creative storytelling in these novels has sparked debates among literary critics, yet they continue to engage and fascinate audiences.

Belle's influence extends beyond the written word, permeating other forms of art and theater. Plays and stage productions based on her life have brought her story to life, allowing audiences to experience the drama and horror of her actions in a communal setting. These performances often emphasize the emotional and psychological aspects of Belle's character, providing a deeper understanding of her complexities. Visual art has also been inspired by Belle's story, with artists creating haunting representations of her and her victims. These artistic interpretations capture the dark essence of her crimes, evoking a visceral reaction from viewers. Cultural events and exhibits dedicated to Belle Gunness offer a more interactive experience, allowing the public to engage with her story through various mediums.

The enduring fascination with Belle Gunness can be attributed to several factors. The intrigue of her unsolved fate continues to captivate those who ponder whether she truly perished in the fire or escaped to continue her murderous ways. Her complex psychological profile adds another layer of interest as experts and amateurs alike seek to understand what drove her to such extremes. Belle's crimes also challenged societal norms and perceptions of women, forcing society to confront the uncomfortable reality that women, too, could be capable of unimaginable violence. This defiance of gender expectations makes Belle's story particularly compelling for feminist true crime readers, who see in her a dark reflection of the struggle against restrictive societal norms.

This element of ambiguity is key to Belle's lasting appeal. The idea that she may have outsmarted authorities and disappeared feeds into a larger narrative of the criminal mastermind who is always one step ahead. It also mirrors similar stories of infamous criminals like D.B. Cooper, whose fates remain unresolved. This unresolved tension is a common thread in many true crime narratives, offering readers and viewers a sense of participation as amateur detectives, piecing together the clues and forming their own conclusions.

Belle Gunness's impact on popular culture is a testament to the enduring power of her story. Each new adaptation, whether in film, television, literature, or art, adds another layer to the legend, ensuring that the tale of the Murder Farm remains a chilling and captivating part of our cultural heritage.

LESSONS LEARNED AND MODERN REFLECTIONS

The chilling discoveries at Belle Gunness's farm highlighted significant gaps in early forensic science, leading to crucial advancements that have shaped modern practices. One of the biggest lessons learned from Belle's case was the importance of crime scene preservation. In 1908, the chaotic scene at the Murder Farm was trampled by curious onlookers, compromising valuable evidence. Today, strict protocols ensure that crime scenes are secured immediately, preserving the integrity of evidence for forensic analysis. Advances in DNA analysis have revolutionized the field, providing a level of precision that was unimaginable in Belle's time. Modern forensic pathology, with its sophisticated techniques and tools, allows for detailed post-mortem examinations, revealing crucial information about causes of death and time frames.

Belle Gunness's case has also contributed significantly to the field of criminal psychology. Her actions have provided a deep well of insights into the study of female psychopathy. Unlike the more commonly studied male psychopaths, Belle's case underscored the unique ways in which female psychopaths can operate, often exploiting societal expectations of femininity to deceive and manipulate. Her story has influenced profiling techniques, encouraging a more nuanced approach that takes gender differences into account. Through Belle, we gain insights into the motivations of female serial killers—how financial desperation, societal pressures, and personal ambitions can intertwine to create a perfect storm of criminal behavior.

Law enforcement practices have evolved profoundly since the early 20th century, influenced in part by cases like Belle Gunness's. Investigative techniques have become more sophisticated, with a greater reliance on forensic evidence and psychological profiling. Multidisciplinary approaches are now the norm, bringing together experts from various fields to collaborate on complex cases. Training and education for law enforcement officers have also improved, emphasizing the importance of understanding psychological factors and the subtleties of criminal behavior. These changes have made it more challenging for modern-day criminals to evade capture and have contributed to a higher rate of solved cases.

Reflecting on Belle Gunness today, society continues to grapple with the complexities of her story. Debates about her ultimate fate remain unresolved, fueling ongoing interest and speculation. Modern true crime enthusiasts are drawn to her story not just for its macabre details but for the deeper questions it raises about human nature and societal norms. Belle's actions defied the expectations of her time, forcing a reevaluation of what women were capable of, for better or worse. Her story serves as a stark reminder of the darker aspects of the human psyche and the ways in which societal pressures can shape an individual's path.

The continued fascination with Belle Gunness's story offers valuable lessons for understanding contemporary issues. As we delve into the past, we gain insights into the present, recognizing patterns and behaviors that transcend time. Belle's story is more than a historical curiosity; it is a lens through which we can examine the enduring themes of gender, power, and morality. Her tale encourages us to question our assumptions and to look beyond the surface, seeking to understand the deeper forces at play.

As we move forward, the legacy of Belle Gunness serves as a poignant reminder of the importance of vigilance, empathy, and understanding in both investigating and preventing crime. Her story is a testament to the complexities of human behavior and the intricate web of factors that drive individuals to commit unthinkable acts. It is a call to continue refining our methods, broadening our perspectives, and deepening our understanding of the human condition. The lessons learned from Belle Gunness are not just historical footnotes; they are guiding principles for the future, shaping the way we approach crime, justice, and human behavior.

CONCLUSION

As we come to the end of our journey through the dark tale of Belle Gunness, it's essential to reflect on the path we've traveled together. From the rugged landscapes of Selbu, Norway, to the smoky streets of Chicago, and finally, to the grim fields of La Porte, Indiana, we've delved deep into the life and mind of one of America's most notorious female serial killers.

We began by exploring Belle's early years, understanding how her childhood in Norway shaped her psyche. The harsh realities of poverty and strict family dynamics laid the groundwork for her complex personality. Her immigration to America marked a turning point, where she transformed from Brynhild Paulsdatter Storset into the cunning and manipulative Belle Gunness. The Murder Farm in La Porte became the stage for her gruesome deeds, where she lured wealthy men with promises of love and prosperity, only to end their lives mercilessly.

Throughout the book, we examined the gender dynamics and societal norms of early 20th-century America. Belle Gunness defied these norms, using her femininity as a weapon and manipulating societal expectations to her advantage. Her actions challenged the perception of women at the time, forcing society to confront the uncomfortable reality that women could be capable of extreme violence and deception.

We also delved into the forensic challenges of the early 1900s, highlighting the limitations that allowed Belle to evade capture for so long. The lack of advanced forensic techniques and the rudimentary state of crime scene investigation hindered the efforts of law enforcement. However, Belle's case serves as a stark reminder of the importance of continuous advancements in this field, offering hope for future crime prevention.

The psychological profile of Belle Gunness provided insights into her mind, revealing traits of narcissism and psychopathy. Her financial motivations and manipulative tactics painted a picture of a woman driven by greed and a desire for control. By comparing her to other notorious criminals, both male and female, we gained a deeper understanding of the complexities of her character and the broader implications of gender in criminal behavior.

As you reflect on Belle Gunness's story, consider the ways in which societal pressures and expectations can shape, and sometimes distort, human behavior. Belle's actions were influenced by her environment, personal experiences, and the cultural context of her time. Her story challenges us to question our assumptions about gender roles and the nature of criminality, sparking important societal discussions.

I encourage you to continue exploring and discussing this case. True crime is not just about uncovering the details of a crime; it's about understanding the human condition and the societal factors that contribute to such behaviors. Your engagement in conversations, sharing of thoughts, and delving deeper into the complexities of this and other cases are invaluable. By doing so, you contribute to a broader understanding of the intricate web of human behavior and societal influence, making you an integral part of the discussion.

In closing, Belle Gunness's story is a chilling reminder of the darkness that can lurk behind a seemingly ordinary facade. Her legacy continues to captivate and horrify, serving as a testament to the enduring fascination with true crime. As you turn the last page, remember the lessons learned and the insights gained. Let this story inspire you to look beyond the surface and question the narratives presented to you.

I want to acknowledge the contributions of the many experts, sources, and supporters who helped bring this book to life. Their insights and research were invaluable in piecing together the complex puzzle of Belle Gunness's life and crimes. I also extend my gratitude to you, dear reader, for embarking on this journey with me. Your curiosity and engagement are what make the exploration of these dark tales worthwhile.

Thank you for joining me in unraveling the mysteries of Belle Gunness. May this story stay with you, prompting reflection and discussion long after you close the book.

CONTINUING THE JOURNEY: "MURDER BENEATH THE CROSS"

As we bid farewell to Belle Gunness and her terrifying legacy, our journey through the shadows of history is far from over. In the next installment of *Shadows of the Past*, we'll turn our focus to a scandalous case that shook the foundations of a small community and perplexed investigators for decades—*Murder Beneath the Cross: The Hall-Mills Case*.

This forbidden affair turned unsolved mystery took place in New Brunswick, New Jersey, in 1922. Reverend Edward Hall and his lover, Eleanor Mills, were found brutally murdered beneath a crabapple tree, their bodies staged in a scene that sent shockwaves through the local parish and beyond. While sensational headlines and sordid details captured national attention, the case remains unresolved to this day, with countless theories about who was responsible and why. Was it a crime of passion, or something more sinister?

Join me as we delve into the twists and turns of this infamous case, exploring the intricacies of forbidden love, betrayal, and the ripple effects of scandal. Together, we will examine the impact of public perception, the influence of power and privilege, and the challenges that early forensic science faced in unraveling the truth. Much like Belle's story, the Hall-Mills case raises profound questions about human nature, societal norms, and the darker side of ambition and desire.

I invite you to continue this journey with me, as we step into the murky waters of yet another mystery steeped in intrigue, tragedy, and unanswered questions. *Murder Beneath the Cross* will take you deeper into the complexities of crime and justice, offering insights that are as thought-provoking as they are chilling.

Thank you once again for your continued curiosity and engagement in the *Shadows of the Past* series. Together, we uncover the forgotten, the misunderstood, and the unsolved, shedding light on history's most perplexing and haunting crimes.

BOOK CLUB DISCUSSION QUESTIONS: SHADOWS OF THE PAST - BELLE GUNNESS

GENERAL THEMES AND STRUCTURE

1. **What was your overall impression of Belle Gunness's story?**
   - Did you find her narrative compelling, and were you surprised by any specific aspects of her life or crimes?
2. **How does Belle Gunness's story challenge societal perceptions of women during the early 20th century?**
   - In what ways did Belle use her gender and societal expectations to her advantage? How does this challenge traditional roles of women in crime narratives?
3. **The book examines both Belle's life and the broader societal context of her time. How did the historical and cultural background influence her actions?**
   - What societal factors—like gender roles, immigration struggles, or the American Dream—do you think played a significant role in shaping Belle's motivations?

CHARACTER ANALYSIS

1. **What do you think were the primary motivations behind Belle Gunness's actions?**
   - Was it purely financial gain, or do you believe there were deeper psychological factors at play?
2. **How do you interpret the relationship between Belle and Ray Lamphere?**
   - Do you believe Ray was a willing accomplice, a manipulated pawn, or somewhere in between?
3. **Belle's psychological profile points to traits of narcissism and psychopathy. How do these characteristics manifest throughout her life?**
   - Can you pinpoint moments in the book where Belle's manipulation or lack of empathy is most evident?
4. **Compare Belle Gunness to other historical figures mentioned in the book, such as H.H. Holmes and Jane Toppan.**
   - How do their motives and methods differ or align with Belle's? What psychological factors set them apart?

FORENSICS AND INVESTIGATION

1. **How did the limitations of early 20th-century forensics and law enforcement contribute to Belle's ability to evade capture for so long?**
   - If Belle's crimes were committed today, how do you think modern forensic science and investigative methods would change the outcome?
2. **Discuss the unresolved mystery of Belle's fate.**
   - Do you believe she perished in the fire, or do you lean toward the theory that she faked her death and escaped? What evidence or lack thereof supports your theory?

MEDIA REPRESENTATION AND GENDER DYNAMICS

1. **The media played a significant role in shaping Belle's legacy. How did sensationalist headlines and early journalism influence public perception of her crimes?**
   - Do you think modern media would portray her story differently? How might today's media focus on her gender, her crimes, or her manipulations?
2. **Discuss the broader societal implications of how female serial killers are portrayed compared to their male counterparts.**
   - How did the media's focus on Belle's femininity and role as a mother contrast with their portrayal of male serial killers? How does this gendered narrative influence the public's understanding of female criminals?

PSYCHOLOGICAL ANALYSIS AND CRIMINAL BEHAVIOR

1. **In what ways did Belle's early life in Norway shape her personality and eventual criminal tendencies?**
   - Do you believe her upbringing, financial struggles, and experiences as an immigrant contributed to her eventual turn to crime, or was she predisposed to such behavior?
2. **The book delves into psychological profiling and compares Belle to other notorious criminals. How has your understanding of female psychopaths evolved after reading this?**
   - What are the key differences between male and female serial killers, and how do societal expectations of gender play a role?
3. **Discuss the psychological and sociological factors that might have driven Belle to commit her crimes.**
   - How do elements such as financial desperation, power, and control come into play?

LEGACY AND REFLECTION

1. **Belle Gunness's story has had a lasting impact on true crime literature and popular culture. Why do you think her story continues to captivate readers and historians today?**
   - How does her story resonate with modern audiences, and what lessons can be drawn from her life?
2. **What ethical dilemmas does Belle's case raise, both for law enforcement and for journalists who reported on her crimes?**
   - How should we balance the need for public awareness of crimes with the risk of sensationalizing or distorting the narrative?
3. **The conclusion encourages readers to reflect on the broader societal implications of crime, gender roles, and morality. What were your key takeaways from the book?**
   - How has this story changed your perspective on societal pressures and how they influence human behavior?
4. **How do you think Belle Gunness would be perceived in today's society, given advancements in gender equality, forensics, and criminal psychology?**
   - Would her crimes be understood differently today than they were in the early 1900s?

LOOKING AHEAD

1. **In the context of the "Shadows of the Past" series, how does Belle Gunness's story set the tone for future cases you might explore?**
   - What parallels or contrasts do you anticipate in future books about other unsolved mysteries?
2. **If you were to recommend this book to others, what specific aspects would you highlight as the most compelling or thought-provoking?**
   - Which sections or themes do you believe would spark the most engaging discussion in a book club setting?

REFERENCES

BELLE GUNNESS AND TRUE CRIME

- Belle Gunness - La Porte County Historical Society Museum. https://laportecountyhistory.org/exhibits/belle-gunness
- Belle Gunness: The Early 20th Century Female Serial Killer You Probably Haven't Heard Of. A&E Real Crime. https://www.aetv.com/real-crime/belle-gunness-the-early-20th-century-female-serial-killer-you-probably-havent-heard-of
- Belle Gunness Murder Farm: Topics in Chronicling America. https://guides.loc.gov/chronicling-america-belle-gunness-murder-farm
- Murderpedia: Belle Gunness. https://murderpedia.org/female.G/g/gunness-belle.htm
- The Truth About Belle Gunness' Lover and Accomplice, Ray Lamphere. Grunge. https://www.grunge.com/474524/the-truth-about-belle-gunness-lover-and-accomplice-ray-lamphere/
- What Really Happened to Belle Gunness, Serial Killer and Mystery. A&E Real Crime. https://www.aetv.com/real-crime/belle-gunness-murders-serial-killer-mystery-butcher-of-men-hells-princess
- Summary of *Hell's Princess: The Mystery of Belle Gunness, Butcher of Men* by Harold Schechter. https://newbookrecommendation.com/summary-of-hells-princess-the-mystery-of-belle-gunness-butcher-of-men-by-harold-schechter/

FORENSIC SCIENCE AND HISTORICAL METHODS

- A Brief History of Forensic Investigation. Universal Class. https://www.universalclass.com/articles/law/history-of-forensic-investigation.htm
- Forensic Science During the Early 20th Century. https://forensicshistory.wordpress.com/2015/01/26/forensic-science-during-the-early-20th-century/
- Visible Proofs: Forensic Views of the Body: Exhibition. National Library of Medicine. https://www.nlm.nih.gov/exhibition/visibleproofs/exhibition/views.html
- Developments in Forensic DNA Analysis. PMC. https://www.ncbi.nlm.nih.gov/pmc/articles/PMC8457771/
- Evaluation of Postmortem Changes. StatPearls. https://www.ncbi.nlm.nih.gov/books/NBK554464/
- Arson Forensics Sets Old Fire Myths Ablaze. NPR. https://www.npr.org/2011/11/19/142546979/arson-forensics-sets-old-fire-myths-ablaze

PSYCHOLOGICAL AND CRIMINAL PROFILES

- Making of a Monster: Belle Gunness. Health Psychology Consultancy. https://healthpsychologyconsultancy.wordpress.com/2013/01/08/making-of-a-monster-belle-gunness/
- Psychopathic Killers Often Hide in Plain Sight. *Psychology Today.* https://www.psychologytoday.com/us/blog/wicked-deeds/201702/psychopathic-killers-often-hide-in-plain-sight
- Psychology May Help Explain Why Male and Female Serial Killers Differ. *Penn State University.* https://www.psu.edu/news/research/story/psychology-may-help-explain-why-male-and-female-serial-killers-differ/
- Egger, S. A. (1990). *Serial Murder: An Elusive Phenomenon.* New York: Praeger Publishers.
- Douglas, J. E., & Olshaker, M. (1995). *Mindhunter: Inside the FBI's Elite Serial Crime Unit.* Scribner.

HISTORICAL CONTEXT AND GENDER DYNAMICS

- Women in 1900. History Learning. https://historylearning.com/the-role-of-women-1900-1945/women-in-1900
- MacKinnon, C. A. (2000). *Feminism Unmodified: Discourses on Life and Law.* Harvard University Press.
- The Norwegians: Immigration and Relocation in U.S. History. Library of Congress. https://www.loc.gov/classroom-materials/immigration/scandinavian/the-norwegians
- Norwegians - Encyclopedia of Chicago. http://www.encyclopedia.chicagohistory.org/pages/911.html

MEDIA AND POPULAR CULTURE

- How Newspapers Covered the Belle Gunness Murders. Newspapers.com. https://blog.newspapers.com/belle-gunness-murders/
- Media Representations of Murderous Women in America. Utah State University Digital Commons. https://digitalcommons.usu.edu/cgi/viewcontent.cgi?article=7806&context=etd
- 6.3: Journalism in the Early 20th Century. LibreTexts. https://socialsci.libretexts.org/Bookshelves/Communication/Journalism_and_Mass_Communication

NOTABLE COMPARISONS: H.H. HOLMES AND OTHERS

- Murder Castle: H.H. Holmes, Chicago World's Fair & Layout. History.com. https://www.history.com/topics/crime/murder-castle

- Jane Toppan: Murderpedia. https://murderpedia.org/female.T/t/toppan-jane.htm
- Axeman of New Orleans - Wikipedia. https://en.wikipedia.org/wiki/Axeman_of_New_Orleans

ABOUT THE AUTHOR
ELIZA HAWTHORNE

Eliza Hawthorne is a historian, writer, and relentless seeker of the past's darkest secrets. Her particular fascination with unsolved cases from the early 20th century has driven her to dedicate her career to uncovering stories that history tried to leave behind. Her work, a blend of rigorous research and a passion for storytelling, breathes new life into the forgotten and unresolved mysteries of yesteryear.

Eliza's *Shadows of the Past* series doesn't just tell stories; it invites readers to step back in time and experience these unsolved cases firsthand. Each book meticulously reconstructs the circumstances surrounding these chilling cold cases, exploring the facts and cultural and social landscapes of the times. Through meticulous research and captivating narrative, Eliza brings the bustling streets of 1910s New York and the quiet, eerie Midwest to life.

While little is known about Eliza's personal life, her dedication to uncovering hidden truths is unmistakable. She is a private person, preferring to let her work speak for itself. Her work speaks to a deep fascination with the power of secrets, the fragility of memory, and the enduring allure of mysteries that defy explanation. Some speculate that Eliza has spent time traveling to archives, libraries, and even abandoned locations tied to the cases she explores. Perhaps it is this hands-on approach that brings a sense of authenticity to her work, allowing readers to feel as though they are on the hunt for answers alongside her.

Eliza's approach is not just scholarly; it's deeply human. She doesn't just chronicle events; she brings the people involved to life—the victims, the suspects, the investigators, and the communities who lived in the shadow of these crimes. Her books often include new theories and insights drawn from her own investigations, challenging readers to reconsider long-standing assumptions and look at the cases with fresh eyes.

For Eliza, the past is never fully gone; it lives on in the stories she tells and the mysteries she unravels. Through her *Shadows of the Past* series, she offers readers a chance to walk the fine line between history and mystery, fact and speculation, and to immerse themselves in the haunting allure of the unknown.

When she's not writing, Eliza can often be found wandering through dusty archives, sifting through old newspaper clippings, and connecting the dots of history's forgotten puzzles. Her work is an invitation to all who share her passion for the enigmatic and unresolved—an opportunity to step into the past and follow the trail wherever it may lead.

ALSO BY ELIZA HAWTHORNE

SHADOWS OF THE PAST SERIES

- The Vanishing Heiress: The Unsolved Disappearance of Dorothy Arnold
- The Silent Witness: The Unsolved Murder of Mary Rogers
- Whispers from the Murder Farm: The Case of Belle Gunness: Inside the Mind of America's Darkest Femme Fatale

ALSO BY PUBLISHER CORDOVA CONSULTING
AUTHOR - KIMBERLY BURK CORDOVA

LEADERSHIP SERIES

- Turning Chaos into Gold: The Alchemy of Women's Leadership
- The Emotional Intelligence Advantage: Transform Your Life, Relationships, and Career

TRAVEL SERIES

- Santa Fe Uncovered: A Local's Insight into the Heart of New Mexico
- Santa Fe: A Local's Enchanting Journey Through the City Different
- Denver Dossier: Themed Adventures for Every Traveler

EMPOWERING SMALL BUSINESSES SERIES

- Artificial Intelligence Unleashed: An Entrepreneur's Guide to Innovation
- Augmented and Virtual Reality: Unlocking Business Potential for Entrepreneurs

- Cybersecurity for Entrepreneurs: Safeguarding Your Business from Online Threats
- The Entrepreneur's Edge: A 3-Book Compilation on AI, Cybersecurity, and AR/VR